Glenn's Sister

A Memoir

by

Carolyn Plath

ISBN: 978-1-7354999-3-2

Library of Congress Control Number: 2022909615

Published by Benicia Literary Arts
P.O. Box 1903
Benicia, California 94510
www.benicialiteraryarts.org

Founded in 2012, Benicia Literary Arts encourages reading
and writing in the community by producing events, creating a community of writers and readers, encouraging their
development, and publishing their works of poetry, fiction,
and non-fiction.

Editors: Mary Eichbauer, Lois Requist, Linda Hastings
Book Design: Jan Malin, Canyon Rose Press
Proofreader: Sherry Sheehan

Contents

Preface

Carolyn Plath should be writing this preface. She wrote this book, but she did not live to see it published. I wish every day that she had. Three of us started working to get it ready for publication before she died, during her last days, with her blessing.

Over several years, Carolyn brought all the chapters of this book to what we simply call "The Memoir Group," a small gathering of women who met (and still meet) twice a month to share and critique our writing. Most of us are working on memoirs, but some bring fiction or poetry to share. Things get "real" in The Memoir Group, and our rule is that nothing shared in the group should be talked about outside. What happens in Memoir Group, stays in Memoir Group.

Carolyn worked long and hard on this memoir. She wrote from the heart about family and friends, about a time in her life when she was her best self—a dedicated caregiver—and yet a time when she put her life and her ambitions on hold and accumulated lasting regrets. Later, when she was, in her own words, "the last one standing," she knew she had to tell this story, not only to honor the memory of Glenn, her beloved big brother, but to sort out the threads of her own life from his and discover meaning in the path she had followed, was still following.

Sometimes Carolyn would read a chapter to the group and her voice would falter, choked into silence by tears. Tissues would materialize from around the table, and someone else would take the papers from her hands and read the chapter to its end. These events, these losses, still had an immediacy for her after all the years, an immediacy that sometimes brought the rest of us to tears along with her.

This is how Carolyn began the preface she never finished:

> I wanted to write a book about redemption. Okay. That is not exactly true.
>
> I started out with the question that Glenn always answered at the end of his stories. He was a great storyteller! And I don't think it was just the pot. In a room full of hippies laughing their asses off over nothing much, he could command the room. When he took the floor, we all listened. And even now, almost 40 years later, we're still retelling his stories and missing him.
>
> One thing that made him so great at it was his self-effacing nature. He always took the pratfall. He made himself the butt. He got the comeuppance. He revealed his foibles and left us with the same takeaway time after time: "That's why I am the way I am!"

I began to wonder why I am the way I am. And maybe, can I be redeemed?

The natural answer for me was that I am the way I am because of the people who have influenced me. So, as a start, I decided to write about my mom, and my dad...and Glenn. Each is noteworthy. But just like back in the day, Glenn took over, compelling me to write about him. To tell his stories. To be like him. Or at least to try. That's where the redemption comes in. Maybe by telling Glenn's story, I can somehow be redeemed.

The elemental mystery of family—Freud called it "the Family Romance," the intertwined complex of love and resentment that binds a family or drives it apart. Parents, children, siblings linked by love, affection, lies, and secrets, spoken and unspoken. The child takes it for granted, soaks it all in. Later, the questions come, and sometimes there are no answers. Sometimes a secret lurks at the heart of a family, a secret with the power to destroy lives. Glenn, Carolyn's big brother, the victim of their family's secret, became her role model. Glenn, the storyteller, the one who wasn't afraid to take a pratfall. The one who loved life so much that, when it became a misery, wasn't afraid to leave it. To reach the truth of Glenn's story, Carolyn had to "channel" him—to speak, in her own voice, the things that happened to him from his point of view without relinquishing her own.

During the process of editing, of trying to honor Carolyn's wishes for this memoir, questions arose, but she wasn't here to answer them. The three of us did our best, pooling our memories, sorting through Carolyn's writing and notes. But the story remains in Carolyn's distinctive voice, with her dry humor and sharp wit.

Each of us feels Carolyn's loss deeply. She was smart, funny, and caring—a warm and generous friend. She and her husband Robert gave great parties and included everyone they knew. A red carpet was rolled out for their annual Oscar party on the night the awards were handed out. Their Fourth of July celebrations took place outside, in view of the beautiful Carquinez Strait, filled with music, and laughter, and friends.

We could not have finished this labor of love without the encouragement and practical help of Carolyn's husband Robert Plath, or the moral and emotional support of the rest of the Memoir Group: Cynthia Black, Tamar Enoch, and Lisa Wrenn. Sherry Sheehan's eagled-eyed proofreading was invaluable. We much appreciated Benicia Literary Arts Board's acceptance of the manuscript and their whole-hearted support. Thank you to them all.

Mary Eichbauer
Linda Hastings
Lois Requist

Prologue: Through the Ether

I keep several pictures of Glenn and me here, on the desk where I write. The closest shows the two of us posing in front of an aluminum Christmas tree. I am about 16 years old, in heavy mascara and white lipstick—the ghostly, pre-goth mode of the day—looking at someone off camera with a warm smile. Glenn—19 or so, healthy, clean-cut, a bit of his edginess starting to show—looks straight into the lens. I like to think of him this way: direct, confident, game for whatever might come.

My all-time favorite photo is of the two of us when he might have been three years old and I was only six months or so. We are propped up against a ruffled pillow in a photographer's studio. It is clear he thought this was to be his photo shoot—right up until they plopped me down next to him. I am full of glee and lurching for the camera. He has folded his arms and sits with a stoic pout, understanding that this is the way it will be from now on, his baby sister stealing the spotlight. A similar snapshot taken about three years later shows the two of us on the concrete front steps of our house in North Tulsa. I am hugging him around his bare mid-riff and he's pushing my face away. Always makes me laugh. Even then, in spite of himself, I know he loved me.

***

I was born in Hillcrest Medical Center. That institution stands on swells of Bermuda grass amid mature elm trees and weeping willows not too far from downtown Tulsa. Any shady spot was welcome and appreciated, especially in June, so the hospital had another appeal apart from necessity.

My mother and I stayed in the maternity ward, on the fourth floor. I am told Momma's mom, Grandma Maddux, was there, and Momma's sister, June, whom everyone in the family called Teetum. I guess my daddy was there too, though his name did not come up in the retelling. But in my version, he is down the hall in the waiting room with the other expectant fathers, reading the Tulsa *Tribune* and tapping his foot impatiently. That is how I like to imagine him.

Little children were not allowed in the maternity ward, so Grandpa Maddux and my brother Glenn stayed on the lawn below. Grandpa and Glenn were the best of friends, and the hospital grounds provided one more setting for them to relish each other's company.

A swing set and teeter-totter offered pastimes for them that morning in June, Grandpa steady and patient, with nothing but Glenn and the green grass and the breeze on his mind. Glenn ran and played and rolled down the hill, returning to Grandpa's arms each time.

Then, I am told, Glenn stopped playing and looked up and called out to the building, "Where's my baby sister?"

Grandpa knew the maternity ward was on the fourth floor, so he pointed to the windows for Glenn to see. He wrapped one arm around Glenn's middle, and they pressed their cheeks together and looked along the length of Grandpa's other arm, following his finger to be sure they were looking at the very same spot. "There she is," Grandpa told him. "She's up there."

Glenn had been thinking of me, trying to imagine me, much as I try to imagine him now. *Where's my big brother? Up there?*

Who can explain the secrets held by members of a family in knowing silence? The confusion and consternation when the secrets come out. The hurt.

I am Glenn's sister. I am the only one with the where-withal to tell his story. Not insignificantly, I'm the only one left standing.

Momma might have told it, but she would not have done. After all, she died so she wouldn't have to face what she saw coming. Extreme? I suppose, but I can see the logic, for a mother. Her picture, also here on my desk, is one I took of her in the car, the colors gone to sepia. Her expression an enigma, she looks to the distance with a Mona Lisa smile.

Daddy? No. No. Daddy wouldn't have done it. He might have told his own story. Okay, that's harsh. Daddy did some surprising things. But tell Glenn's story? No.

So, it's on me to tell the story for Glenn. Maybe it's my story too. We'll see. I know it's been in me, waiting to be told.

In our family, we did not say "I love you." None of us did. Not Glenn and me. Not Momma and me, nor Momma and Glenn. Certainly not Momma and Daddy!

From the outside you might have thought us disconnected or unconcerned with each other, an odd lot of marbles knocking around in the lid of an old shoebox. But that is not the truth of it. Sure, there was not much hugging or patting on each other or words of encouragement—or discouragement, for that matter. Just that after Daddy left, we knew—Momma, Glenn, and I—that we were the nugget, the core, the essence of life and learning, of survival, each for the other.

And though Momma and Glenn and I did not display our affection, we had an understanding—an appreciation you might say. We went about our business; Momma watched us and listened to our points of view, looked us in the eye, with pride in that appraisal. I do not think we ever let her down. She liked it that we followed our own minds even if, on occasion, we drew a sidelong glance.

Now, I find that I loved them with a fierceness I did not recognize within me. Except Daddy. Not that I did not love him. I did and I do. I simply remained in the second ring of his orbit. He offered no approach point. Or, more likely, I was, as children can be, obtuse, naive to the obvious. Maybe he did not know what to make of me and so we both proceeded with caution. And, always, that secret was there between us, between him and Glenn.

"Where's my baby sister?" Glenn wanted to know. And I, newborn and wrinkled and swaddled in my mother's arms, heard him through the ether. In the marrow of my bones, I heard him.

Chapter One

Little Glenn & Grandpa

Glenn had his own stool at Grandpa's workbench. An infant's highchair really, with the food tray removed and two added layers of the same red paint that coated the barn. After Grandpa retired, they tinkered away mornings and afternoons in the dingy light of the tool shed. They repaired the chicken coop and set a trap for the possum that kept stealing eggs.

Grandpa carried Glenn, or Glenn ran alongside him with a hammer and a pocket full of finish nails. When Grandpa pulled the combs from the beehive dripping with honey, Glenn was the first one to get a chunk of wax to chew, the first whose taste buds surged at the burst of liquid sweetness. Grandpa brushed Glenn's hair back with his thick, gnarled fingers and told him to always keep a big forehead.

The first grandchild, Glenn delighted the family. Round and robust, he enjoyed the loving gazes of Grandpa and Grandma, Momma and Teetum. He laughed and ran from one to the other. Each would sweep him up in gleeful hugs, releasing him to run to the next. If we set music to the scene, it would be Mozart. Light. Light. All light.

But when Glenn ran to Daddy, the music changed. Daddy had that cloud. That angry cloud. I wonder if he was happy before Glenn was born. Maybe it was Glenn's button nose and hazel eyes that put my daddy off his good cheer for the next thirty years. I wonder if he ever held Glenn, or if he always regarded him stiffly with that grim down-turned mouth and heavy forehead.

No one treated Glenn differently except Daddy. All the rest loved him and cared for him and played with him and included him totally and without reservation. But perhaps, on occasion, the adults exchanged a knowing glance above the children's heads. Maybe Momma had a tell-tale thought when she swept him up and away from Daddy's indifference. Teetum may have let a grain of self-righteousness seep through when she babysat him. They must have emitted their knowledge on the etheric plane.

And Glenn received those signals. He knew.

But none of that mattered because Grandpa had enough love and pride to make up for any slight. Grandpa did not care about anything except that this was his grandson, his boy. And, so, Glenn flourished.

I did all right too, able to take so much for granted. No need for me to question the subtext. But I made note of it in the casual way any child recognizes her own status, her own privilege.

So many years later, I visited Grandma and Grandpa's house on the west side of Tulsa when I heard it was to be torn down. I felt like Alice in Wonderland after she took the pill that made her 10 feet tall. Tiny would be the only word for the house that held so much meaning for me. Tiny. Flimsy. The rooms were laid out with no hallway; each one opened onto the next in succession. Living room to bedroom this way; living room to kitchen, that. Only a cramped alcove with a mop and galvanized bucket set the bathroom apart from the kitchen on one side and the second bedroom—the one where I dreamed of getting up to pee and instead wet the bed.

I felt like an Amazon in the living room where Glenn and I grew up with our silent sibling connection, playing side-by-side, not speaking, but communicating just the same.

When Grandma immersed herself in the New Testament, underlining passages with her ballpoint pen or making notes in the margins, I would slip into their bedroom and open the drawers to the cabinet where she kept her jewelry—hat pins and brooches, beadwork necklaces and matching clip-on earrings, her Eastern Star medallion and Grandpa's Masonic ring.

If she went into the kitchen to start a cake, I had time to pull the knob on the heavy door to her closet until it swung open, weighted by an extra over-the-door loop that held her full-length mink coat. With square shoulders and straight, cuffless sleeves, it gleamed in the low light of her museum of church dresses, stoles, plumed hats, and shoes. I lifted and touched each piece with reverence. Her pheasant-feathered pillbox hat was my favorite. The iridescence! And a net! Tiny knots in fine, tough thread to wear over your face. Such mystery!

Soon though, the silence would catch Grandma's ear and she would call out to me, "What are you getting into?"

"Nothing," I would call back, the child's lie.

"Well get out of it!"

So, I would step back, push the door into place, and return to Glenn on the living-room floor. He would smile up at me and shrug. Caught again, but it did not matter. Admonitions here were gentle, not like at home with Daddy, where fear was the motivator.

In truth, we did not suffer at home. Not exactly. Daddy never hit Glenn and he hit me only once. We did as we were told, without hesitation and without argument. No wheedling allowed.

Daddy established this feat of parenting via intimidation. He was big and dark, after all. Six feet, six inches tall. Black hair and the dark eyes of a raptor. No need to search for signs of pride or vulnerability when he looked at us—those sentiments would not be found. I guess things had not worked out to his liking, and he spent evenings mulling this over from his corner of the couch. Probably he suspected Momma of machinations but could not quite prove it. And, since she was guilty, she likely do-si-doed around his pointed questions, avoiding confrontation. Glenn and I danced too.

Daddy resented watching us if Momma had to leave the house for an evening meeting at school. He read the paper, or a magazine about shooting his guns or one about flying airplanes. Do Not Disturb. Once, on such an evening, the phone rang and I answered. Teetum asked, "Where's your momma, Carolyn Sue?"

She says I answered without hesitation, "She's gone to the goddammed PTA!"

Bedtime was finite. Stop what you are doing and go. Lights out. Go to sleep.

I knew this, but somehow, I asserted myself, just once. Momma enrolled me in the Audubon Society and my new book was full of wonder—real creatures that lived in a world I would never see. So, when Daddy told me to go to bed, I closed the book with a finger between pages of shore birds and swished down the hall on the balls of my feet. I hopped into bed and resumed my happy survey. The Great Blue Heron! Could there be such a bird?

I must have lost myself because, suddenly, I heard Daddy close in the hall! Oh no! He will kill me! He will take my book! In a flash, I tossed the book over the side of bed next to the wall, away from the door. But the light was on. I was caught.

In that instant, Daddy appeared in my doorway. He filled the frame. "What are you doing?" he said, as he approached my bed, controlled, deliberate.

"Nothing."

My heart pounded. I must have tugged at the covers because he took the corner of the sheet and flung it and the bedspread back, expecting to see proof of my mendacity. But nothing was in the bed but me, my T-shirt nightie, and my spindly bird legs. Confused by this, he studied my face. He did not like being fooled. He took my shoulder, turned me to the wall, and spanked my skinny butt. One hit. He turned away and flipped the light switch as he left. "Go to sleep!"

It didn't even hurt. Just the shock. The insult. I never tried to fool him again. Well, not for a long while anyway.

Glenn was more adept at subterfuge. Or maybe it was just that Daddy did not watch him that closely. Daddy's apathy worked in Glenn's favor. And Glenn did not strive for Daddy's attention like I did on occasion. He did not seem frustrated or sad, perhaps because Grandpa filled the vacuum. But Daddy's sullen neglect worked on him just the same. He seemed to accept that his daddy did not love him, but over time, the question arose. For me it was idle curiosity. Glenn began to wonder why.

Chapter Two

Abadan & the Aftermath

Daddy took a job "overseas"!

We got dressed up, better than for church even, and flew around the world on TWA. After New York, the flight to London was so long that Glenn and I slept in a compartment overhead—where carry-on luggage goes now—with pillows and blankets and its own air conditioning vent. From there to Paris and Stockholm and Munich, criss-crossing our way to Copenhagen, Damascus, and on to Abadan. A new round of vaccinations awaited us at every port-of-call, so many that when I recognized the scenario about to play out, I rebelled and hid from the needle under a table in the doctor's office. No doubt my crying gave me away and I was stuck again.

At each stop, maybe as consolation for the endless inoculations, Momma bought me a souvenir doll: a gypsy woman with a coin necklace, a Swedish milkmaid. Glenn got pocketknives with iconic images on each one. We lined up with practiced smiles for Daddy to take our picture, in front of Big Ben, the Arc de Triomphe and the Umayyad Mosque.

We lived two years in the white sunlight of the Iranian desert while Daddy helped build a refinery on the southern border, the shore of the Persian Gulf—Abadan. Glenn and I played within the walls of the compound and swam in the company pool. Glenn went to the company school with the other ex-pat kids. His second-grade class picture shows him smiling at the end of the row, his shirt buttoned wrong, hanging askew. I was kindergarten age, but they had no kindergarten, so I stayed home with Mom and Majid, our houseboy.

We kept rabbits, and I spent many days chasing baby bunnies and catching lizards. I learned to ride a two-wheeler on the flat and dusty road next to our house. Majid, a deferential young man, shopped and cooked and cleaned up for Mom. He put his brown hand on top of my head, talked softly to me and laughed gently, as adults do, when I cried and ran from the dinner table after he confirmed that this slow-simmered stew, the main course of our meal, was made up of Pinky, our momma rabbit.

Daddy bought a motorcycle, an Indian, for his daily commute. He kept it in the hallway of the house, newspapers underneath to catch drops of oil from its crankcase. It clicked and sighed as it cooled down after his evening ride home from the plant and gave the house a petroleum ambiance. We had to be careful not to brush against its blistering tailpipe when we passed by. Momma must have lost any discussion about securing it outside. When she sidled past it on her way to the back of the house at night, she tightened her jaw and flattened her lips.

When Daddy's assignment in Abadan ended, we returned to the United States flush with the per diem and bonuses of his "foreign service." Their frenzy of buying went like this: Momma and Daddy got a brand-new car each—a 1957 Mercury Turnpike Cruiser for her, baby blue and white with air-conditioning and electric windows all around, and a two-seater, a 1957 Corvette for him, low and fast, and loud! And a new house—first owners—on the booming east side of Tulsa, Wagon Wheel Addition, 112th East Avenue.

New furniture. I don't know if Mom decorated that house to her taste, or by what was first in her view when she had Abadan money in her hand. We had "blonde" furniture, as she called it. I guess now it would be called "Scandinavian." Plain. Straight lines. Sharp corners. Veneer.

She accessorized with a display of artifacts from our time in Iran: copper bowls and serving trays with intricate etched designs, carved wood camels and elephants and boxes with ivory inlay holding elaborate silver jewelry she never wore. And all of it overshadowed by The Dancing Girl. Daddy had picked her out. She was woven into a lustrous velvet rug. We said it was a tapestry.

Momma called her "Dahncing Girl."

On a flying carpet six feet long and four feet tall, the Dahncing girl spun her sultry spell from a street in Tehran. Her sky was sapphire blue, the ground and nearby buildings earthen tan. Her dark hair was bound by a band across her forehead with a teardrop ruby suspended between her eyebrows. A veil covered all but her piercing eyes, lined in black. Her breasts, swathed in twisted cloth, swelled above her naked belly. And the vee at the waist of her silky pantaloons dipped below her navel. With cymbals on her slender fingertips and gemstones on her bare toes, she swayed above us, on the wall next to our dining-room table.

When Daddy was home, the house harbored a dark, viscous aura. After work, he read the newspaper in the living room across from Dahncing Girl. With the drapes drawn he sat silent and unapproachable in the perpetual dusk of the room. Mom moved about in a wary state. She and Daddy did not exchange knowing looks or engage in playful jesting. I must have catalogued their distrust of each other, their wariness, but that onion remained unpeeled. I would never have asked Daddy why. And as for Momma, I was on her side.

Glenn and I worked the periphery, did as we were told, kept quiet. Daddy liked us to be quiet. We remained mute at the dinner table. We had to clean our plates, and no food could be rejected without at least one bite. Glenn devised a scheme for spitting the required taste of any offending food into his napkin; thus, he met his obligation to try it without actually eating it, escaped detection, and abandoned me to my principles. Rather than eat a spoonful of beets, for example, I chose to sit alone at the table, all family and dishes cleared away—save me and my place setting—until bedtime.

Once, after a terrified struggle for self-control, I passed gas during dinner. Momma turned in my direction and Glenn looked at me as though I'd pulled the pin from a hand grenade. We waited while Daddy studied me with disgust. "You need to go to the bathroom," he said. I left the table mortified and did not return to my meal.

Years later, when Daddy was married to Sheila, her son Willie, my new step-brother, put a whoopie cushion under the pad of Daddy's chair at the kitchen table. When Daddy sat down, he was the one who emitted a loud, ridiculous gaseous blast. I caught my breath and waited for the grenade to blow, but to my amazement, Willie laughed, and Sheila laughed, and Daddy, though not truly mirthful, fought a smile, shook his head, and said nothing. Nothing at all.

One day, Daddy brought me an apron with an embroidered hem. Of all things! It made no sense, and it made me unreasonably happy. Anxious to show him how much I loved that stupid doily, I worked my knees onto the cushions next to his corner at the farthest end of the couch. I touched the newspaper he held spread to its full width between us. "It has pockets! Look Daddy!"

He tilted the paper toward me so he could make steely eye contact. His level gaze held me immobile. "Yes, Carolyn. I got it especially for you because it has pockets." He snapped the paper back into place. He didn't see Momma roll her eyes, or the shake of her head as she held out her hand to me and turned back to the kitchen. I went with her and wore the apron, now devoid of its appeal, as I set the table for another family dinner.

I heard only one fight. In the night—I should have been sleeping. Maybe I was, but woke to the unfamiliar tenor of their voices, the strain in the atmosphere. I waited for more, my body arching in their direction, but only a charged silence followed. And footsteps. A door.

That weekend I played down the block in the front yard of Dorothy Nell Jetton's house when the Corvette's engine growled. I turned to see it lurch backward onto the street. As Daddy came toward us, I grinned and held Dorothy Nell's white bunny up for Daddy to see, but when he slowed the car and leaned down to signal his departure, he looked so sad! Is my daddy crying? Why does he have all those shirts in the car? I watched his progress down the block until the bunny started kicking and had to be let go. I ran home to Momma, but her door was closed. Must be another migraine.

Divorce. I guess. He just didn't come back. A vacancy at the table. A corner available on the couch. More silence.

And he took the Dahncing girl with him! When I asked Momma, she snapped, "Good riddance!"

Chapter Three

Roller Coaster Road

Grandpa was a company man, a Texaco man. He and Grandma bought a house on the west side of Tulsa, just one block from the refinery gate. He walked to work every shift for 37 years. He came home for lunch every day; when he worked nights, Grandma left a "lunch" for him on the kitchen table. He ate alone under the yellow light of the incandescent bulb overhead.

Grandpa's only son, my Uncle Jesse Jr., worked at the refinery too. And so did my daddy. Maybe that's how Daddy met my momma, through her brother Jesse Jr. at the refinery, but I'll never know for sure. They're all dead now. There's no one to ask.

Maybe that's how Momma's sister, Teetum, met A.L. He was a company man too.

***

Daddy strode up to the door of Grandpa's house, taking the stairs in twos. The house was dark, but the porch light was always on. He rapped on the door, disturbing the moths on the screen. Lights came on immediately. Grandma came to the door in a white cotton gown with her braid draped over her shoulder, wisps of red hair creating a halo against the backlight. "Roy? What is it?"

"I need to talk to Jess," he said, and she let him in.

Grandpa came into the crowded living room with his hair oily and disheveled. It was 5:00 a.m. He'd been off the night shift a long time.

They sat, Daddy on the couch with the floral throw, his elbows on his knees and great head hanging. Grandpa waited in his chair.

My daddy raised his head with tears in his eyes and looked at Grandpa. He swallowed and wiped his nose and looked down again. Grandma stood in the doorway that led directly from the living room into their bedroom. They waited.

At last, Daddy raised his head again. He spoke in that low tone, that flat, even tone. "A.L. is molesting Carolyn. Tammy too." Grandma put her fingers to her lips. "He's a filthy degenerate son of a bitch and I'm going to kill him."

"Now let's wait a minute," Grandpa said. "How do you know this?"

"Carolyn told me. Jesse told me about Tammy so I asked Carolyn and she told me."

The men fell silent. Grandma shifted her weight then decided to sit. She gathered her gown underneath her and pulled her knees and ankles together.

Then Grandpa stood and Daddy did too. Grandpa disappeared into the bedroom and came back holding his

20-gauge shotgun by the barrel, a green and red box of shells in his other hand. His hair was combed and he wore a plaid flannel shirt and dungarees.

"We'll catch him when he comes down for dinner."

They got into Grandpa's green Plymouth and drove the block down to the refinery gate. They parked on the side away from the streetlight, across from where the wives sometimes waited to pick up their husbands after a shift.

Teetum drove up and parked. She had chicken in wax paper and potato salad in a Tupperware bowl, all in a brown bag on the seat of their Chevrolet. Grandpa got out of his car and walked over. Teetum cranked the window down.

"Git on home," he said.

"What? Why? I've got A.L.'s dinner."

"Give it to me and git on home, girl. Now do it." She started to speak and chose not to. She slumped back in the seat for a moment, then sat up, handed him the bag, turned the key and took the steering wheel. She put the Chevy in gear, eased away from the ditch, and rolled out of sight, tilted onto the shoulder, gravel crunching under the tires.

Grandpa returned to the Plymouth and, within minutes, A.L. appeared, walking slowly toward the gate house, the hem of his overalls sagging, dragging, frayed by the asphalt. He took a final pull on his cigarette and dropped it still burning as he walked. His bald head caught the glow of light as he turned out of the gate, looked left, then right. No Teetum. Where's my dinner?

Grandpa started the Plymouth and spun a quick U-turn, lining the passenger door up with A.L. Daddy swung the door open and got out, forcing A.L. to step back. "Get in."

"Wha...? What's this?" A.L. said. Daddy hit A.L.'s shoulder hard with the heel of his hand. Again in that low, flat tone, but insistent, "Get in!"

A.L. got in and Daddy got in the back behind him. Grandpa looked sideways at A.L. "Shut up," he said. "Just shut your mouth." A.L. knew he'd better.

Grandpa turned onto 21st Street and drove out to River Road. About two miles in, he turned off River Road onto what we called Roller Coaster Road, an unmarked dirt and gravel lane that split huckleberry thickets and elm trees. No more streetlights.

They traversed one hill after another until they were about midway through the undulating landscape when Grandpa abruptly stopped, threw on the parking brake, and said, "Get out of the car."

"You gonna leave me *here?*" A.L. said, opening the door.

Daddy was already out of the car. He shoved A.L. and A.L. stumbled away. "What have you done to my daughter?"

"Nothin'! I ain't done nothin' to your daughter! What are you talkin' about?" A.L. said in a mock show of confusion.

Daddy shoved him again and this time A.L. fell. He got up and took a step toward my daddy. "I don't know what you mean! I love that girl! I'd do anything for her."

"Shut your filthy mouth! Don't you ever say a word about her!"

"But..." Daddy shoved him again and A.L. fell again. Before he could get to his feet, Daddy turned and pulled the shotgun from the car. He broke it open and slung it over his forearm as he'd done so many times at the range. A.L.

stayed down and Daddy got the box of shells, flipped it open with one hand. He set it on top of the Plymouth and pulled two shells from the box.

A.L. began to whimper. "I'm sorry! I didn't mean to do it. I cain't help myself! It's a sickness!" Snot began to run from his nose to his lips.

"Get up," Daddy said without inflection. Grandpa stood by.

"No!" A.L. said, struggling to his feet. "Roy, don't do this! I never meant to hurt her. I didn't hurt her."

"You'd better shut your mouth, A.L.," Grandpa said, his voice flat and even too. "You ain't helpin' yourself."

Daddy plunged the shells into the breach and snapped the barrel into place. A.L. blubbered, his shoulders shuddering. "I won't do it again. I won't…I won't…I swear…"

Daddy brought the gun up to his shoulder in a swift movement, like he practiced at the range. He put his cheek on the stock and took aim, only he didn't say "pull." He just waited until A.L. looked up. When their eyes met, Daddy squeezed the trigger and the massive boom repeated and repeated, echoing along the valleys of Roller Coaster Road.

Daddy and Grandpa stood over him for a moment while the energy of the gunshot retreated. Daddy spit. It landed on A.L.'s hand. Grandpa spit on the wound and went around to the trunk of the Plymouth. "Let's get him in here."

"No," Daddy said, "this is good. We'll just move him and cover him up." They each took an arm and pulled A.L. farther and farther from the gravel road. The gulch narrowed and the brush thickened and that's where they let him lie with his arms still over his head, like a scarecrow on the run.

They took his shoes and his wallet and his wedding ring, worked their way through the brush back up to the car, and they drove away.

From there they went to Teetum and told her A.L. left town and not to ask again. She didn't ask. She looked around like the beaten dog she was and saw the upside. She slept well that night and after that most every night. When the plant called to ask about A.L., she said he ran away. They called again and she said no, she hadn't heard. Didn't look like she was going to, but she would let them know if she did. Or she'd tell him to call in.

***

That was my fantasy for the longest time. I based it on the facts as I knew them.

But A.L.'s still alive. He's the only one of that generation still alive. Ironic. They're all dead and he has Alzheimer's so bad he doesn't remember any of it. He acts like he never did anything to me, but he did. Here I am still muddling through it decades later and he's happy as can be. Probably wonders why I'm so cold.

When Jesse told my daddy what A.L. was doing to me, Daddy and Grandpa didn't kill him, but they took him and the shotgun out to Roller Coaster Road and threatened to; he left me alone after that.

Up until then, I had kept our ugly secret. I never said anything until Daddy came to me, and I guess I never would have. That's how I came to be known as "The Mouse." I just shut up. At family gatherings, when A.L. was around, I kept my chin tucked and my eyes down and said nothing.

I stayed out of reach lest he pull me onto his lap like he did Tammy.

In those years, I made only a nebulous connection between the abuse I endured and the gifts Teetum gave me and my cousin Tammy. She said she'd always wanted a girl, that was why she bought us girly clothes and bows and shoes with dainty socks. After her death, I began to wonder if she was somehow trying to make up for her own willful ignorance, her eye turned elsewhere, her ear made deaf when we needed most of all to be heard.

And then there is her schizophrenia. Did she break and splinter because her conscience could not take her complicity? Her cowardice? Better to go crazy than to own up? What's a little electroshock therapy compared to the truth?

It was Tammy who spoke up—that's how it came to light that A.L. molested not only the two of us, but also my other cousins and multiple kids he came into contact with as a Little League coach. When A.L.'s oldest son had two daughters who sometimes stayed with him and Teetum, Tammy tipped them off to protect the girls. A.L. went to McAllister State Penitentiary for it.

He never apologized. Teetum came to me once, after A.L. went to McAllister, to say he told her of all the kids he abused, he felt worst about me. I wanted to puke. That's what made me special? Gosh, thanks. When he got out of prison, he tried to act like nothing happened, like he was my uncle and I was his niece. But I didn't have to pretend any more. We didn't have a secret.

I've heard it's bad karma not to forgive, but I don't know how to go about it.

Sometimes I picture him on his hands and knees, groveling in front of me, begging my forgiveness. I can say the words then, in that fantasy. But all I really know is that he's going to die without acknowledging what he did to me. He will go to hell, which is good, since he's lived in the protection of his dementia, the only one among us who doesn't know the damage he's done. How he left a little girl feeling soiled and ashamed. How that becomes step one for her in any situation: convincing herself that she matters; that in spite of all that, she is as valuable as anyone else.

Even now, these decades gone by, he lingers, like a bad smell, putrid. Where is that coming from? Oh yeah. Big A.L. Never can get rid of that stink.

Chapter Four

Daddy Never Learned to Say "No"

After the divorce, my daddy took me places. He'd never done that before, and so now I began to learn about him, fit him into my puzzle of the world. Each new observation, every fresh experience, served to widen my view and formulate my assessment of the way things were in his world and how things were for me, and Momma, and Glenn.

Daddy took me to the practice range where he shot clay pigeons: 100 in a row, 150, 200 without a miss. He wore a vest with patches on it proclaiming his prowess with a shotgun.

We drove out to Harvey Young Airport where he kept his plane, a Piper Cub J-3, a two-seater. I watched him while he tinkered with it and gave instructions to the mechanic, Manuel. Daddy called him "manual," like a book.

He flew me to air shows where we watched stunt planes do snap rolls and barrel rolls and hammerhead stalls. He knew some of the pilots. They talked about *gs* and ailerons while I leaned into his leg.

When we flew, I sat in the front seat of the Piper and he worked the stick from the tandem seat behind me. I still couldn't see over the dash except up at the sky—white with clouds, indecipherable.

Once, on a trip back from Kansas, when it came time to switch to the reserve tank of gas as he'd instructed me to do, I turned the lever too far, past the notch he'd shown me, and soon, starved of fuel, the engine began to sputter. In an instant Daddy threw off his seatbelt, surged over my seat back and clicked the lever into its proper place. Replenished, the engine returned to its droning, we leveled out and flew toward home, our hearts racing.

My daddy stood six feet, six inches tall. I had to skip and hop to keep up with his long stride. He always got attention, and I did too, when we were together. "You gotta run to keep up, huh, Little Lady?" a man might say when passing us on the sidewalk. At the 7–Eleven, the cashier flirted with him by flattering me. "What a pretty little girl! Those blue, blue eyes!"

When this happened, I put my chin on my chest. No one taught me how to accept a compliment. But Daddy would smile. No one had taught him how to say no.

Daddy's Corvette was a 1957 hard-top convertible. He unlatched the hard top and we lifted it off the car and onto the front porch. It was heavy for me, but I could do it. Then we drove with the sun in our faces.

Daddy had aviator sunglasses, like James Bond. If we passed other Corvettes, he lifted two fingers off the steering wheel in acknowledgement. Other drivers gave us a wave in return.

The Corvette was a two-seater, no room for anyone else. Glenn didn't go. He didn't go to the practice range or the airport. I wondered, but never asked, why he wasn't included. We could have squeezed him in.

Very early one summer morning when I was nine, Daddy parked at the curb in front of our house with a suitcase and a foldout Texaco map of the USA. Mom had packed a bag for me. Daddy and I were going to California to see Grandpa and Grandma!

Daddy put my bag next to his in the Corvette's trunk and a pillow on the console. When I settled into my red leather bucket seat, Daddy expanded the road map and stretched it across my lap. "Here we are," he said pointing to Tulsa. "And here's Grandma." His big hand slid left as he dragged his finger west along Route 66 to Los Angeles. "Make sure we don't get lost!"

I could only smile.

He turned the key and the Corvette's throaty rumble said, "Excitement!" He revved the engine a couple of times and we waved at my mom on the porch, he with his left hand and a half-smile, head tilted down to see her; I with my right hand and roller-coaster grin. That must have been Glenn in the shadow behind her, the screen door obscuring his expression. He turned away when Daddy revved the engine again and eased off the clutch. We crawled away from the curb and accelerated down the block.

My brother Glenn was named for Daddy's best friend Glenn. We stopped at Big Glenn's house that morning.

"Wait here," Daddy said and swiveled. He folded each long leg up to his chest, then out of the car. Big Glenn opened the screen door and smiled, his teeth too large and too perfect, as Daddy strode up the walk. When they came out a few minutes later, Daddy had something wrapped in a faded blue towel under his arm.

"See you in a couple of weeks," Daddy said to Glenn, as he reversed the process of managing his legs to get back behind the wheel. Glenn leaned down and smiled at me. "Say 'hi' to your Grandma!"

"Okay," I said. The prospect thrilled me.

Daddy lifted the pillow and put the towel-wrapped object on the console underneath. The frayed edge of the towel fell open to reveal a handgun, a square looking one, an automatic.

"Don't you worry about that; it'll keep us safe," Daddy said. "Don't touch it either. It won't bother you under the pillow."

He gunned the Corvette's engine, and this time we leapt away from the curb, down the block, and onto the road toward the highway.

Turned sideways in my seat to nap as we drove, I rested my head on the pillow. I could feel it there, the gun. I didn't worry about it. I knew we were safe. Once, in my sleep, I pushed my hand under the pillow. When my fingers bumped the hard metal, I woke and sat up in one motion, looking at my dad, fearing he'd know I touched the gun. "Hey," he said with a rare smile. "Did you sleep?" I nodded.

"We're leaving Oklahoma."

I opened the map and he pointed to the Texas panhandle. Then he hunkered over the steering wheel and said, "Scratch my back?" I always obliged.

We pressed on through Amarillo toward Tucumcari, left the pale yellows of Texas and took on the ruddy reds of the New Mexico desert. Once we saw a coyote as he ambled away from the highway. He turned as he went and threw an accusatory glance over his bony shoulder. Dusk gathered as we climbed up through the Sandia Mountains. At the crest, Albuquerque stretched twinkling before us.

Daddy and I smiled at each other. I remember feeling pleased by this, and even then, I made a mental note of the occurrence—two smiles in one day. Daddy liked being on the road.

"It's been a long time since lunch," he said. "Let's find something to eat and a place to sleep tonight." I sat up tall and straightened my shirt.

Soon, we turned off the highway into the gravel lot of the Star Cafe. "Eat," its neon sign commanded. The Lobo Motel, "Gateway to the Sandia Crest," sat next door. We locked the Corvette and went toward the cafe lights. People turned when we appeared, the giant and the little girl. Daddy directed me to a booth, its green vinyl cold against my skinny legs.

Our waitress's name tag read "Darlene." She came to our booth immediately with menus in her armpit, utensils folded into paper napkins in one hand, and two plastic glasses filled with ice water in the other. Somehow she sat it all on the corner of the table, handed us our menus, and pulled a damp cloth from her forearm. She leaned across the table and made sweeping motions with the cloth, wiping away nothing, her breasts hanging low.

Darlene's hair was mostly blonde and pretty stiff. Her bangs made a cylinder on her forehead. Her skin was smooth, her eyes clear brown with black liner and mascara, and her lips orange sherbet to match her uniform.

She smiled at my daddy and said, "You folks been on the road awhile?" I guess it showed.

Daddy smiled back, "Six this morning."

"Let me get you some coffee—or, will you stay the night?"

"We'll stay," he said.

"Then decaf it is," Darlene smiled again. "Would you like a Coke, sweetie?" I nodded yes and she turned away.

Daddy watched her go and I remembered a time before the divorce when he and Momma and Glenn and I were all in the Turnpike Cruiser after watching *Up Periscope!* at the Admiral Twin Drive-in Theater. Daddy drove us across the street to the A&W Root Beer stand. A girl there, a carhop, took our order for root beer floats and turned to go. Daddy watched her too.

"I want to be a carhop!" I chirped.

"Your butt's not big enough," Momma replied flatly.

***

Darlene returned with my Coke and Daddy's coffee, a sugar bowl, and a little metal pitcher full up with cream.

"What are you hungry for?"

Daddy ordered chicken-fried steak, mashed potatoes, brown gravy, and green beans. I had a grilled cheese sandwich and French fries. We ate in silence. I sucked my shiny fingers between each bite.

"How 'bout some pie?"

Daddy looked up to see Darlene cock her hip and tilt her head. "We've got apple, cherry, pecan, coconut cream, and lemon meringue." No question. We would have lemon meringue.

Our wide slices of yellow custard arrived with stiff white meringue two inches tall. Darlene gave us fresh forks and we dug in. She lingered near the booth for a moment. "Good, huh?" We both nodded and smiled.

She moved to the booth next to ours, leaned over it and wiped more nothing from the table there. "So...you're headed out in the morning?" she ventured.

Daddy didn't answer right away. He watched her while he finished a bite of crust. He seemed to measure her and his response.

"Yeah, I hope I'll be able to sleep tonight."

She smiled and turned toward the cash register. Daddy watched again for a moment then smiled to himself as he returned to the sweet tang of lemon custard.

We checked into the Lobo Motel and Daddy moved the Corvette in front of Room #3 facing the gravel lot. Twin beds and a TV on a rolling stand. The rabbit ears had aluminum foil crumpled onto them. Daddy sat on the end of his bed and took off his enormous shoes. He set them aside and curled his back like he did in the car when he wanted me to scratch it.

"Get into your pjs and get in the bed." I hoped we could turn on the TV, but I wouldn't ask. We would watch TV if

Daddy wanted to. I took my toothbrush into the tiny bathroom and changed.

When I came out, Daddy was stooped over the TV turning the dial from channel 3 to 4 to 6. He wiggled the antenna at each new setting with no appreciable effect. A snowy picture showed an Albuquerque newsman reading his script. Different channel, different newsman.

I got under the stiff white sheets and propped the scratchy pillow behind my neck. Daddy stretched out onto his bed; his feet extended past the foot of it. He wrestled his pillow a bit too and focused on the newsman. The volume low, the newsman's report monotone, like Daddy's voice. He stared at the screen. There would be no conversation and soon I fell fast asleep.

***

A click and another click woke me. The room was dark except for the fluttering glow of the test pattern on the TV screen, a black-and-white segmented target with a line drawing in the center of an Indian chief in profile. Just then the door opened, and in the widening rectangle of light from the Lobo Motel's exterior, Daddy's lanky silhouette emerged. He was coming in.

I shut my eyes and pretended to sleep. He closed the door without a sound and turned toward the room. He sat on the end of his bed again and turned the TV off. He undressed in the dark and got under the covers in his underwear. Soon his breathing became slow and regular.

He woke me the next morning with a shake of my shoulder. He was already dressed. "Let's go," he said. I knew to get up right away and get started no matter how groggy I felt.

We stepped out of Room #3 into a cool and damp first light. Two red pick-up trucks and a tan VW camper angled toward the windows of the Star Cafe. Fluorescence glowed from inside brighter than the fledgling dawn around us.

We crunched across the gravel of the parking lot into the cafe and sat at the counter this time, reflecting our need to get back on the road. Sharon, a squat waitress in the familiar orange-sherbet uniform, brought water, a ceramic coffee mug, and menus. I looked around for Darlene.

Daddy saw me looking and seemed to understand my unspoken question.

"She works nights," he said.

Chapter Five

No More Grandpa

Momma and Daddy swept us out of bed in the dark of night with few words—"Get up. We're going to Grandma's."

We watched, foggy headed, as Daddy zipped up his jacket and left the house before I could begin to wonder what he was doing there. The Corvette's engine growled to a start, disproportionately loud in the still, wee hours. We could hear him surge down the block and as he turned off our street and onto the main road.

We didn't even get dressed. Momma hustled us into sweaters and put on one of her own. We hurried onto the wide bench seat of her Mercury Turnpike Cruiser, still too boggled to ask why. She leaned forward over the steering wheel as though it would help her see farther than the headlights allowed and ferried us to Grandma and Grandpa's house across town and down from the refinery in West Tulsa.

Under the amber light of Grandma's living room Glenn and I played by rote. This wasn't right. Something wasn't right. Momma was grim. Teetum was grim. Grandma's house in the dark.

We played in our pjs and sweaters without interacting. We brushed our arms across the dense rug, pushing miniature trucks and planes without laughter or conflict, imaginations stilled. We waited and listened in that hollow space children hold for uncertainty.

A white dawn broke when Daddy's Corvette pulled into Grandma's dirt and gravel driveway; the headlights' glare flooded the space, faded the wallpaper. A pause, then Grandma came through the front door and hesitated, pale, disheveled, bereft. Daddy stood behind her.

We all looked up, suspended between before and after.

Grandma looked at each of us, then said, "Ain't got no more Grandpa."

The air went out of the room and her knees buckled. Daddy caught her by the armpits and swung her into her chair. She slumped forward and her thin shoulders wobbled under her gown and sweater.

Momma made coffee and we huddled around Grandma. When it got lighter, Teetum called the courthouse where she worked. "This is June," she said. "And my daddy died. Okay. Okay. Okay. I'll call you back." She put the phone down and we huddled up again.

Momma didn't go to her teaching job, and we didn't go to school that day. I felt surprised and wondered why. Oh, because Grandpa died. That's what you do; you stay home from school. Then what? When I went back, would the other third graders know why I had missed? Would they stand and stare at me like the kids in the horror film *Children of the Corn?* Were all their grandpas alive?

Glenn and I stayed close to the adults that day, but heard their words from far away, as though through a fever. And we could see there was no more Grandpa.

At his funeral we sat as if wrapped in a dry fog, our legs dangling from the pews of the First Baptist Church of West Tulsa. We could not know what any of this meant and hardly knew a question to ask past what Grandma had already explained—ain't got no more Grandpa.

For me, Grandpa's death opened a curious kind of vacancy. No big man to sit me on his lap and pare off sections of Red Delicious apple, peel them and feed them to me as though I were an expectant koala. No one to tickle me past breathing. No one else had a nub where his little finger had been before the buzz saw got it. No one to wiggle a nub at me like he did to make me squeal. But I had Momma and Teetum and Grandma still. And while Daddy often seemed stiff and judgmental, he would sometimes say, "Carolyn," and when I turned, he'd study my face and tell me to hold still so he could take my picture, on a pillow in my bathrobe, knees tucked under, watching TV. Then he would smile the faintest of smiles.

But for Glenn, Grandpa's death was global. It signaled a shift in the topography. For him, the horizon was obscured; the sunlight dampened; the ground no longer lay level under his feet. Oh, he had Momma and Teetum and Grandma too. But Grandpa was gone and Daddy didn't call his name. Daddy didn't take his picture. Daddy didn't look at Glenn.

Chapter Six

Sheryl & the Kiss

After the divorce, our life on 112th East Avenue stood in contrast to Daddy's single life of sports cars and airplanes. To his credit, Daddy never missed a child-support payment. His $150 a month and Mom's teacher's salary kept the three of us afloat in bologna and cheese and Chef Boyardee.

Mom bought an upright piano from Westside Baptist Church for $50. It stood against the dining-room wall where Dahncing Girl had been and soon was cluttered with a vase of plastic flowers on a doily at one end, sundry knick-knacks, a hairbrush, and a cat toy at the other end. Tattered hymnals appeared, and Mom would sit on the bench and play with dramatic flair "Gladly the Cross-Eyed Bear" or "Onward, Christian Soldiers." I sat next to her, so happy. I tried to read the music, but mostly I watched her fingers pounce on the keys as we sang and sang loud. With exuberance and abandon. It felt so good to sing.

Maybe I asked for piano lessons on a bad day; maybe it was the end of the month. Mom snapped, "Why don't you ask your dad?" Confused by this, I never asked him or her again.

Mom took in a renter to help with the bills—Sheryl. She moved into my room and Glenn and I became awkward roommates. At 12, I was an embarrassment to his worldly 15. We stretched a strip of masking tape the length of the floor down the middle of the room, one twin bed on each side. And because we were delighted by Sheryl and the light she brought to mom, we maintained a tenuous accord.

Sheryl was young and blonde and pretty and fun. Kind to me, she seemed to know my state of uncertainty and need. She taught Spanish at Nathan Hale High School, the same school where Glenn cut classes and where Mom taught geometry and algebra and dumb-dumb math. At the end of each day I crossed the playing fields between my junior high and the high school to meet Mom and Glenn. Now, sometimes Sheryl and I would wait together after school. I always felt happy to be with her, as if I could be pretty and smart, too. She listened to me.

When Sheryl lived with us, we had parties and handsome young men came to drink beer and laugh.

Once, on a suggestion from Sheryl, she and Mom planned a Budweiser party, a "beer bust." As part of the preparations, Sheryl wrote to Anheuser Busch asking for party favors. To everyone's surprise and delight, they sent coasters and napkins and a billboard-scaled poster showing bottles of Bud the size of bowling pins and giant happy drinkers clinking their beers above a table spread with hors d'oeuvres and olives as big as footballs. We got a stepladder and tacked the poster up, covering three walls of our L-shaped living room and dining room, ceiling to floor.

The night of the party, all manner of people I didn't know came to stand in our house, eat potato chips and onion dip, and drink Budweiser, screwdrivers, and Bacardi and Coke. Lamps glowed amber inside and windows and doors stood open to the balmy night. LPs stacked on the turntable dropped and spun against each other; the diamond needle scratched out songs from Elvis, Nat King Cole, and the Fabulous Ink Spots.

After a cursory pass-through, Glenn stayed in our room with a plate of party fare and his guitar. I watched the party from the dark of the hallway and developed a crush on a man with dark hair and blue eyes. He winked at me and said, "Hey Lucy! Is this your kid?"

Unaccustomed to the gaze of a man, I shrank into the shadows, only to re-emerge and watch again. Everything was unfamiliar and thrilling.

Soon, I realized my mom had stepped onto the front porch, so I slipped across the corner of the living room and through the screen door to see her. She sat on the steps next to a man I didn't know. Sheryl and another man faced them, sitting in nylon-strapped aluminum lawn chairs on the sidewalk below. I positioned myself one step down from my mom and leaned my chest onto my bony knees. I picked up a stick and traced it along the concrete, listening.

The adults talked. In the spell of that warm Oklahoma night, their expressions were new and the cadence unfamiliar. Gestures had to be taken in, nuances deciphered. They knew I sat there, but talked around and over me, putting on a show without acknowledging their audience. When they laughed, I smiled, not knowing why.

Once, in unison, Sheryl and her friend paused in their laughter and tipped up their bottles of beer, pulling and swallowing, their pulsing throats exposed. In the silence, I turned, expecting to see my mom drinking too, but instead found her kissing the man beside her, a deep, open-mouthed kiss. I watched. My mom. The man with his tongue in her mouth.

When they separated, a short silence settled around us. I looked at my toes and the "Who Loves You Baby?" pink polish I had applied that morning. It was already cracked and ragged. I picked at my little toe.

"Well," said Sheryl. "It's a good party, don't you think, Carolyn?"

"Yeah," I said, glancing at her and then at my mom. "Yeah."

In the next moment, I got up to go. Mom handed me her paper plate with crumbs and residue clinging to it. I took Sheryl's too. Inside, I wove through the partiers unnoticed. The man with the blue eyes and black hair didn't see me, though I passed close enough to tug his sleeve. He stood with his hand low on a woman's back. They smiled about something.

In the kitchen, I took a few chips and some onion dip, a Coke and a few green olives, and made my way back to my room. Glenn must have slipped out. His guitar lay on his rumpled sheets. I settled onto the middle of my bed and flipped the pages of my *Seventeen* magazine, skimmed past "How to Find Your Special Style," and "Fashions for a Boy-

Meets-Girl Summer." I paused to study the starlets, glamorous girls in sparkling dresses. They looked back at me from the photos, their cool confidence evident and taken for granted. Brooke Shields. Cheryl Tiegs. They had what I did not. I tried to imagine being their friend. We could talk only about them and that would be okay with me. Better, in fact. Best. Yes, that would be best.

On the next page, the article brought me to a full stop: "After the Party—Should You Kiss and Tell?" The experience of watching my mom kiss that man, that stranger, came back to me. Cross-legged on my bed, I could see her, see them. Their mouths, their eyes, their throats.

The advice of the article was "no," of course. You should never kiss and tell. So I didn't ask my mom about it. I didn't want to put her in an awkward position. Or me. I wanted to protect myself too.

I didn't want to think about it. But I did.

Chapter Seven

Albuquerque

I remember being surprised the first time Momma talked to me about going to college. I was a senior in high school and had skipped so many days of school—29—that my school counselor, Opal Lloyd, called me into her office and let me sit and watch her scalp shine through her thinning hair while she reviewed my attendance records line by line. She ticked off each absence, put a total at the bottom and circled it, then looked up and studied me, perhaps checking off items on her internal list of my shortcomings.

"If you miss one more day of school, you will not graduate," she pronounced. She paused and watched while I processed this information. "Do you understand?"

Most days Patti Lee, Joanne, Tina and I left campus innocently enough, just to go to lunch. We'd pile into Duane Dooley's canary yellow '67 Chevelle. (Duane was the too-nice guy Patti Lee dated—he let her have the car all the time.) Patti Lee let me drive since I was better at a stick shift. We dashed east down 11th Street to Shake-a-Go-

Go. Service was quick and the burgers juicy. We had only half an hour to get there, eat, and get back into our seats for afternoon classes, so precision was a must.

But some days—I guess it was 29 of them—on our way through the parking lot we started to talk about Randy Padgett, or Billy Joe Johnson, and the next thing you know, we'd be driving west on 11th Street, onto I-44, and across town to Boots Drive-In, or to cruise Thomas Edison HS, or Nathan Hale HS, in hopes of getting a glimpse. Those days we might never get back to school.

"Carolyn?" Mrs. Lloyd was tapping her ballpoint pen on the earpiece of her bifocals.

"Yes. I understand."

Thus ended my adventures in class-cutting and boy-watching.

***

Maybe, being a college graduate herself, Momma had pictured me in college all along. But if she did, she never said so. And I never heard the story of how, or if, she'd been encouraged by Grandma and Grandpa, or by her school counselor, to go to Northeastern State Teacher's College. But she did, the only one in her family—siblings or cousins, parents or grandparents—to go on past high school, let alone earn a bachelor's degree and a teaching credential. It set her apart; I could see it. Everyone in the family said she was the smartest, as though it was the education made her smart. When I asked her about it, she said Teetum was the smart one, and I wondered how that could be. Teetum was crazy, after all.

Mom and I talked about sororities once, and she said she'd been a GDI—God Damned Independent. It made her sound angry, but I knew then that I'd be independent too.

I have a picture of Grandma Maddux, Momma's mom, wearing button-up shoes and riding sidesaddle on her way to her first teaching job in Cozahome, Arkansas. She worked there as an assistant to the teacher, a man, in a one-room schoolhouse, until the State of Arkansas required classroom teachers to pass a competency test to keep their jobs. She passed; he didn't—and the job became hers.

***

You could say I went to college with my mom. When I was 13, she enrolled in a graduate program at the University of New Mexico in Albuquerque. It was a program for working people like her. You could complete your master's degree in three grueling summers. Glenn stayed in Tulsa with Teetum and her three boys. And Mom and I loaded up the Mercury and drove 12 hours on Route 66 across the plains of Oklahoma and the Texas Panhandle, into the center of New Mexico, so she could go to school.

She timed the trip so we left Tulsa early evening, drove through the night and topped the ridge of the Sandia Mountains to see Albuquerque in early morning, twinkling below. We surely stopped to eat and to pee, but I don't remember any of that. I just remember flying along the highway at night on the Merc's wide front seat, with my mom behind the wheel. We listened to Wolfman

Jack on Radio XERF, howling across the open miles. We knew all the words to "Puff, the Magic Dragon" and "It's My Party, and I'll Cry if I Want To." We sang along with the Chiffons, "He's so fine! Whoa yeah. Gotta be mine! Whoa yeah. Sooner or later. Whoa yeah. Hope it's not later!"

If the radio waned, we might sit in silence for a mile or two, then Mom would say, "Come on, help me stay awake," and she'd start up the call of "Little Sir Echo, how do you do? Hello!" "Hello!" I responded and we pushed on into the darkness. I imagined how we must look from high above, a matchbox of a car whisking along silently, headlights revealing a bright triangle of road before us.

I stayed in Momma's dorm room at UNM. She must have paid extra. The young women in the hallway smiled when they passed me, but we didn't talk. Why would we? They were graduate students and I was 13, gangly and shy. When Mom went to class, I walked the campus sidewalks from one stucco building to the next, an unseen waif in the pallid landscape of the campus under a white New Mexico sun.

Mom got me a meal ticket for the Student Union cafeteria, so I moved unnoticed among the adults and ate alone, never seeing another child. Once, I took my ham sandwich on white bread out to the steps of the Union and peeled back the cellophane before noticing that I had settled close enough to three young men to hear their conversation. "How was your weekend?" "Good," came the reply. "Played basketball. Had two orgasms."

They were laughing so I doubt they noticed my retreat, quiet but quick. Whatever orgasms were, I felt certain they weren't for me! I headed down the steps and around the corner.

I marveled to find a bowling alley in the Student Union. For days I watched the bowlers before I got the nerve to try it. Knowing nothing but what I'd seen, I hefted the first ball I found off the rack closest to my assigned lane. It was heavy! I mimicked the procedure I'd observed, put my skinny fingers into the hard, hollowed-out holes, held the ball under my chin, and took a wobbly step forward. But when I swung the ball back, I couldn't hold it and wham! It smacked the shiny wooden planks behind me.

I cringed and took a furtive look around. Other bowlers turned back to their lanes. So, I hoisted the ball up to my waist, leaned back to manage the weight of it and worked it around so that I could put my fingers into the holes and got set again. WHAM! Again, even louder.

This time I saw a man turn in my direction and put down his drink. He got up and headed toward me with purposeful strides. "Hi, I'm Buck," he said when he reached my lane.

"Hi," I said feeling small and stupid, keeping my eyes averted. He was a man, a grown man, not one of the younger students who had orgasms on the weekends. Kindness emanated from him. Safety.

"Have you been bowling before?" he asked.

"No."

"May I look at your ball?"

"Okay."

"Whoa! You picked a 16-pounder! No wonder you're having trouble! Here, look, see right here? This tells you the weight of the ball. Let's see if we can find you a lighter one."

I followed him as he turned ball after scarred-up ball along the racks until he said, "Here we go—eight pounds. That's about right for someone your size."

He handed me the ball and I had to smile. "Give that one a try. You'll do much better."

I was glad he didn't stay to watch me, but after my first throw I looked across the lanes in his direction, hoping for his approval. He looked up at just the right moment and gave me a smile.

***

Nights, when Mom was hunched over her calculus, I was as still and quiet as I could be for as long as I could be. I read as much as I could read; worked more puzzles than entertained me; shifted and turned one time too many on my twin bed. She'd glance in my direction, unseeing, but still shake her head as though dispelling an apparition before turning back to her equations.

So, I'd slip down to the dorm's lobby where a baby grand piano gleamed, poised and inviting, in a room with glass walls. I slid onto the bench and plinked and plunked on the keys. I played "Heart and Soul" again and again. I yearned to know how to play something, anything else. Oh! "Chopsticks"! I played the scales with my right hand and spanned the keyboard with both hands, CEG all the way up and GEC back down again, thinking of Liberace and his coattails. More "Chopsticks"; more "Heart and Soul."

Then, I caught a movement at the glass door to the enclosure. A young woman with papers at her chest. Music, I supposed. She could play. She wanted practice time.

I asserted myself for another moment with the scales, then left the bench, eyes cast down.

***

About halfway through the summer, Mom and I tired of our circumstances. I spent my evenings reading, without a sound, on my side of the dorm room across from her. Night after night, she bent over, deep into statistics, a green metal desk lamp hot on her pages of notes. This made an inadequate alternative to our routine at home of easy contentment, leaning against her side in front of Perry Mason and Della Street. Maybe we ate meatloaf sandwiches there on the couch. If I didn't understand what Perry meant by a red herring, or why Lt. Tragg called the Sulky Girl's alibi a ruse, Mom always took time to explain.

When she spoke to me then, I studied the irises of her eyes, olive green, one with a spot, a brown spot, perfectly round and suspended just outside the pupil. Her eyelashes, light and straight. Her red hair, thick and rich at her shoulders, pulled away from her face, open and unpretentious.

She watched me too when she spoke, to see that I understood, her hand on my arm, or she'd brush a strand of hair off my face. When I nodded, we'd turn back to the TV, sure of so many things.

But she was tired now, because of the workload of her intensive program, and the added burden of me, silent, compliant, but still asserting pressure of a kind—*talk to me, look at me, think about me.* By the time I met Vickie, another child of a grad student, Mom must have been desperate for some relief. So, on a blustery afternoon, when I burst into the dorm room full of the news of my new friend and my adventures across campus, calling, "Mom!" She drew a breath and pushed it out before she looked up from her books. She startled me, stopped me, upright in place.

"Carolyn," she said, "don't ever have kids."

Oh. I stepped back. It's okay. I can tell her all this stuff later, at dinner maybe, or before bed.

A few days later, I told her Vickie was leaving with her family for a weekend in Santa Fe. Exasperated at this latest interruption, Mom said, "Why don't you see if you can go with them?"

And so I did.

I walked to the girl's house that evening as her parents were loading their car for the trip north. They barely noticed me lingering there, bashful, unsure how to proceed. At last, Vickie came out with a pillow under one arm and a teddy bear under the other. She made her way to the back door of their car as I approached.

"My mom said to ask if I can go with you," I said. Vickie's social skills were on a par with mine—she stood limp-armed, her pillow just touching the driveway, and looked at me as though I were tinny and flat, two-dimensional. But her mom had overheard. "No," she said, her tone measured as she looked me over. "You cannot go with us." Vickie shrugged.

The rejection enveloped me and rendered me immobile. I watched a moment longer while this family—mother, father, and child—bustled about, finalizing details of their trip, then I turned for the slow walk back to the dorm.

At the end of summer, our return trip to Tulsa did not hold the anticipation of our drive to Albuquerque. Oh, we sang some songs, and the Wolfman howled, but, mostly, we pushed along the highway, Mom with her face forward, purposeful and determined, probably working through her checklist of tasks that awaited her in Tulsa: Make preparations for the new school year of teaching; get Glenn and me ready for our new school years, too; have a life.

I can't say what I might have been thinking as the miles slipped under the Turnpike Cruiser's tires. Maybe I replayed my moments of inadequacy and embarrassment in the piano practice room, or of watching Vickie's family after I'd shrunk to invisible at the edge of their driveway. Maybe I tried to figure out why my mom wanted to get rid of me that weekend. She wasn't going to have an orgasm, was she?

More likely, I was in the moment—hungry, or tired, perhaps uncertain of my future. What I do know is that I didn't think about going to college, or having children, for many years. Glenn never mentioned those things either.

Chapter Eight

Genetics Lesson

The kitchen reflected my adopted philosophy that a good cook cannot concern herself about the mess she makes. Around me lay bowls, sticks of butter, brown and white sugar, baking powder, baking soda, measuring spoons, spatulas, and my mom's stand-up mixer—all of it dusted with Gold Medal flour.

With a vision of my Grandma Maddux in her apron hovering nearby, I poured cake batter into greased and floured pans and smacked each one on the countertop as though I understood the purpose of such actions. I donned oven mitts and placed the pans in the oven. I let the oven door snap shut, set the timer and stood with my gloved hands on my hips, feeling competent and powerful.

Glenn came in as I began to assemble the ingredients for frosting. Without hesitation he swiped the inside curve of the batter bowl with the flat of his right hand, and before I could express my shock, he licked his palm all the way up to his fingertips and smiled a "whaddaya-gonna-do-about-it?" smile.

"Not bad," he said as he picked up the bowl and swung it onto his hip like a mother hoists an infant. "What is this?"

"Cake. It's cinnamon chocolate cake."

"Hey, you've got some batter on your nose."

This would be a first, I thought. Glenn never mentioned my nose without a comment on its length, or its hump, or my witch-like countenance. Skeptical, I reached upward.

"That's right. Wa-a-ay out there on the end of your nose!" Again with the smile.

"Perfect. Thanks for your help. Now leave me alone; I've got to make the icing."

"Nah, I'll stay. This is interesting."

In one move he pulled a vinyl-covered chair away from the kitchen table, swung his leg over its back and straddled it, cowboy-in-the-saloon style, with the batter bowl still cradled in his left arm. There he sat, grinning up at me, cleaning the last of the cinnamon chocolate batter from the sides of the bowl.

"About your nose," he began.

"No! About your nose!"

Suddenly he grew solemn, and I knew I shouldn't have said it. We'd had this conversation before. While my nose was oversized and masculine on my otherwise delicate face, it was clearly a replica of Daddy's nose. No doubt. I was my daddy's daughter.

But Glenn's rounded pug nose was an anomaly in the family. It troubled him.

***

At least once before he'd told me he thought he was adopted. On that summer day he stepped onto the front porch and sat in the shade with his back to the screen door while I sat on the top step, knobby knees at my chest, and tossed my jacks onto the concrete. I bounced the red rubber ball with my right hand and collected one jack at a time into my left.

"What?" I'd said without looking up. "You're not adopted. You're crazy. And you're my brother."

"Who else looks like me?"

I held the jacks, trapped the ball, and fixed a blank stare on his puckish scowl. He had put some thought into this.

"Really. Think about it," he went on. "No one else in the family looks like me. I must be adopted."

I tossed the jacks again, started on twosies, and listened. "People are always telling you how much you look like Mom or Dad. No one ever says that to me."

That much was true. Mom's friends would look from me to her and back again and comment on the resemblance. Once, Mom replied to such a remark with, "Everyone thinks Carolyn looks like me until they see her daddy."

I took all this for granted. And I never questioned Glenn's looks or his place in the family. Maybe our cousin Timmy had challenged Glenn. Ironic, since the whispers about Timmy's lineage worked their way around the perimeter of family gossip at least once a year.

"What does Mom say?"

"I don't know," Glenn said, looking down. A wrinkle formed between his eyebrows.

I took this to mean Mom told him he wasn't adopted, but he was not satisfied. He continued to frown as he dug into his pocket and pulled out a crumpled pack of Swee-Tarts. Unrolling the end, he dumped its contents into his palm—one large pinkish pill. He held it out to me, and I shook my head.

"Last chance!" he said, lifting the candy between thumb and forefinger, smiling now as though he were in an ad for the sour little treat. He placed it on his extended tongue.

I returned to my game. Threesies. Foursies. I didn't know how to ease his uncertainty. I tossed my jacks. Fivesies. Sixsies. He watched me play for a while longer, then stood. This time he extended his foot when I tossed the ball up and tapped it, sent it bouncing down the stairs onto the cracked clay of our front yard. I scrambled down the steps to recover it, and when I turned back to the porch, he was gone.

***

Now, here in the kitchen, I could see him process the family resemblance argument again.

"We learned about genetics and heredity in biology."

"Yeah?"

"Yeah—I've gotta be adopted." He got up and set the bowl on the counter. He licked the last of the batter from between his fingers and said, "I'll be right back."

Moments later he returned with his 10th-grade biology book, dittos frayed at the edges, and notebook paper in the same condition, all wedged into his blue cloth-covered binder. He plopped it on the table and began to shuffle through the assemblage. On a second pass he flipped individual papers from back to front, looking for something specific. At last, in frustration, he opened the book and paged through a chapter midway in, until he came to the chart he remembered.

"Here!" he said and held the open book between the mixing bowl and me.

"Are those pansies?"

"No! Pea plants! It explains about genes and heredity. I have to be adopted."

"You're a pea plant?"

"Shut up. This chart says that two pea plants can only make more pea plants that look like them."

The chart comprised four quadrants. Three had purple pea plants, but the lower right quadrant had a white pea plant. I pointed to it, dropping a little confectioner's sugar onto the page.

"Maybe that's you."

He folded the book shut in disgust.

"No really," I said. "What did it say? 'Recessive gene'? Maybe that's you. You act recessive."

Instead of making him laugh, my comment made him mad. I was supposed to listen. He felt something. He knew something, and even I wouldn't consider it.

"Doesn't matter anyway. I'm not going to live past 30."

"Why do you say stuff like that?"

"I just know, that's all."

He gathered his papers, shoved them and the book back into his binder, just as the timer for the cake began its rasping buzz.

"Oh," he added on his way out, "I'm getting a hearse."

Chapter Nine

Foam Rubber

Glenn took up the gauntlet of brotherly torment and carried it high, as a calling, a duty. He knew I was self-conscious, so he never let me forget my flaws.

His instincts took him to my nose, the thing I hated most. It was Dad's nose, and to my way of thinking, too big for my face, and with a lump to boot. So, at the breakfast table Glenn might say, "Hey, Schnozzle, pass the butter... please." Or if a car honked when it passed us on the way to school, he'd ask, "What? Did you say something?" Then, "Oh never mind. I thought that was your honker!"

If I had a pimple, he made it Vesuvius, ready to blow. He would throw up his arms and cover his head as he running, "Save yourself! Save yourself!"

My arms were feeble; my butt like a banjo; and, as we became teenagers, my chest was like the Bonneville Flats, he said. Like the Texas Panhandle, level as far as you could see. Not a hill in sight.

So I whined and wailed and bemoaned the plane of my chest, and Mom came to my rescue. At JC Penney she and I bought bras, size 32B, with foam inserts so I could at least pretend to have "filled out." I wore them to school the next Monday and thereafter. Those two conical mounds created just enough of a rise to satisfy me, if not fool anyone else who had seen me flat-chested the Friday before.

Soon after, Glenn found the inserts in the laundry and brought them to the door of my room. He held them in place on his chest, looked down at them and laughed so hard his body shook. The weightless pink cups fell from his hands and bounced and wobbled on the floor. He turned away, back curled, and staggered down the hall, doubled up and convulsing with mirth.

Glenn knew his friends were looking at me a little longer than they had before, so he kept my feet on the ground. I think he figured that's what brothers were for. Nevertheless, he waited for me every day after school, smiling his mischievous smile as I approached. He walked with me to his car with his shoulders back and chin just up. We rode together daily, happy and easy, Mick Jagger shouting, "Hey! You! Get offa my cloud!"

Once, Carol Lucas, THE most beautiful and popular girl in the school, asked me how long Glenn and I had been going together.

"He's my brother!" I said.

"Oh!" She was surprised. "You don't look alike."

Her comment meant little to me. I did however make note of it. I added it to my collection of curiosities—a compilation of comments, sidelong glances, and cryptic refer-

ences that flew over my head, but not out of my consciousness. I would come back to them later and turn each one
over, examine it for context and nuance, categorize it and
construct meaning at last. The veil lifted only after all the
facts were in.

***

Our house was the one where Glenn's friends hung out.
They didn't mind that the TV had been broken for three
years, or that we never had Cokes or chips or any food to
offer. But our mom was cool, and it didn't hurt that we always had the house to ourselves for an hour or two before
she got home from her own school across town.

So, after school—if they went to school—Glenn and
Dave, Gordon and the Mentzer twins, would careen around
our corner collected in Glenn's dusty '49 Ford and Mitchell
Henley's shiny '66 Nova, jerk to a halt, and stream across
the red clay and clumps of grass of our front yard and into
our living room.

It was heavenly for me, most of the time, having all those
boys lounging around. I would come out of my room after making sure my Maybelline was laid on thick and my
short shorts were short. I wore white lipstick, even though
Tara's mother, down the street, took a look at me once
and said my face looked like two holes burned in a white
blanket.

Just a year before, I might have slipped into the living
room on my way to the kitchen but sit on the piano bench
instead. The boys would mostly ignore me. Not rude, just
detached. Showing off.

Now, they included me in the conversation.

I hadn't learned to flirt. I hadn't grown up with a man in the house. And, maybe because I didn't have a dad to look at me with a man's eyes, I couldn't believe or see or understand that a boy might be curious about me. Might want to play a little conversational game. My development was delayed, but I caught on. Thanks to Gordon.

"Hey, Carolyn, what's up?" Gordon might ask and wait to hear my answer. A bit soft around the middle and perpetually rumpled, Gordon was the least attractive and the most willing to engage me. And for me, he was the least intimidating. He earned his place among those strapping young men by being smart and funny and level-headed—maybe from being raised by his grandma. He constituted the voice of reason among the others, who were carefree and beautiful and bursting with life.

"Hello Byoo-tocks!" Gordon said when I came into the room. Glenn and Dave, the twins, and Mitchell Henley turned to look from their stations draped across the furniture or stretched out on the floor.

"Byoo-tocks!" Until I learned the word "buttocks," I thought Gordon was calling me beautiful.

"I thought lipstick was supposed to be pink," he said, smiling at the specter of my complexion.

"I don't like pink."

"But isn't lipstick supposed to enhance the natural pinkness of your lips?" he persisted.

"I suppose, if you like pink." Dave smiled and so did Greg Mentzer. It must not have looked that bad.

That's about when Glenn decided that I had had enough of his friends' attention, and they had thought long enough about me. He came over and sat next to me on the bench and rubbed his nose, his turned-up little pug of a nose. I knew I was in for it.

He sneezed and sneezed again, fake sneezes, "Achoo! Achoo!"

I don't know why I waited.

"I wonder why I'm sneezing?" he asked with mock sincerity. The boys straightened up and smiled in anticipation. "Oh, oh! This is bad!" he said, rubbing his nose again and again. "I must be allergic to something around here. Achoo!" He smiled a crocodile's smile.

Counterfeit confusion and dismay. "The only thing I'm allergic to is foam rubber." He looked around at everything but me. "There's no foam rubber in here, is there?"

And then he turned to me. Innocently. "Carolyn?" I stood to go.

The boys arched toward us, their smiles stretched with glee. Then Glenn focused on my chest. My flat chest with the pink push-up pads. My sad effort to look "developed."

I made a move to leave, way too late. His eyes widened, "Oh no! Foam rubber!" He pointed and squealed, sneezed and sneezed. He got up to the hoots and guffaws of the boys. I bolted through the kitchen and laundry room, to my mom's room, and back down the hall, slamming my bedroom door to his phony apology, shouted through laughter, "Come back! Come back, Carolyn! Your secret is safe with us!"

I stood behind the door, breathing and thinking, thinking of Dave, and Mitchell, and the Mentzer twins. Gordon.

Glenn. Their voices subsided and I leaned against the door a while longer. I looked at my chest, the one Mom bought me, two perfect cones, size 32B pyramids. In front of the mirror now, I angled to the side and back to the front. Still better than flat, I thought. Better than flat.

Chapter Ten

Glenn & the Hearse

Glenn wanted the hearse less as a mode of transportation than as a vehicle for expressing his morbid sense of doom.

A 1959 Cadillac Fleetwood funeral coach, it sat low; its wide, white sidewall tires bulged and cracked where they met the concrete. Chrome S-shaped scrollwork stretched along each side of the extended carriage. Its cavernous backspace retained the tracks laid down to guide the departed safely into a locked position.

He'd found a chauffeur's hat on the seat below the steering wheel and wore it when he settled onto the brittle black leather. Already slight, he appeared underage behind the wheel in relation to the size of the hat and the girth of the vehicle. He evinced a certain glee when driving it.

Its suspension was loose, so that when Glenn turned our corner to park, maneuvering became an effort of swerve and recovery. He pumped the brakes, and the unwieldy beast came to a rest at the curb in front of our house with a squeak and lurch. The golden curtains, heavy with the accumulated, clinging, gummy dust of years of silence, swayed out on their rod, then settled back into place across the back window.

The coach's oxidized paint would never shine again. Its substantial grill pulled toward the pavement as though succumbing to the gravity of so many mourners, so many sad journeys. Rusty wheel wells and pitted chrome completed the ambiance.

I stepped out and stood on the front porch next to Mom. She stared across the clay and ragged weeds of our front yard at Glenn and his hearse. "He must have gotten it from Tom Hammer," she said to herself. A shake of her head, barely perceptible from the curb, punctuated her commentary. Glenn, standing next to the driver's side door, grinned at us and patted the peeling vinyl roof.

***

In Tulsa, old Route 66 doubles as 11th Street through town. Rick Hammer's dad, Don, owned one of the thirty or more used car lots on that stretch of concrete and tar. I imagined this span of road to have been part of the Oregon Trail or some other dusty hardpan path through Oklahoma to the Pacific. When covered wagons cracked an axle they stopped here for repairs, or a trade-in. For me, that anachronistic thought explained car lot after car lot and the cache of flattop motels strung along the length of 11th Street, from Broken Arrow at the east end of town, all the way to West Tulsa, Sapulpa and beyond.

Little more than a converted mobile home parked on an asphalt lot with light poles, streamers, and a ragtag array of cars looking for their third and fourth lives, Hammer's Auto Sales provided a source of fascination for Don's son Rick, Glenn, and their merry band. Tom Hammer indulged his son and, it seemed, Glenn, with access to the transitory vehicles of his wayside business. Don drove the newest cars; Rick, the coolest, at the moment a 1960 Impala, black with red interior; and now, if only for a few days, Glenn had his hearse.

By way of celebrating his ghoulish ride, Glenn decided he wasn't going to school Monday. Instead, that morning he took the hearse on a circuit of all the guys whose parents left their houses early. Rick and Dean Hammer lived closest. Tom headed to the car lot early, but Tula, their mom, opened the door in her robe and slippers when Glenn honked the funeral coach's tired horn. She appraised Glenn with skepticism and raised her hands, questioning. Glenn spoke softly from behind the wheel, knowing she couldn't hear, "Can Rick and Dean come out to play?"

She called out to the curb, "What are you doing here? It's early. They're not ready for school. Rick's driving anyway." She scowled, truly suspicious now. So Glenn smiled and waved at her, nodding his head, mouthing "thank you" as he pulled away from the curb.

No point in trying to get Gordon. He had to take his grandma to work at the courthouse downtown. They had only one car, so Gordon left the house with her at 7:00 a.m. each weekday and dropped her off. No matter. Both Dave's parents also left their house every day at seven.

Dave's bedroom faced the street and he was a light sleeper. The flat tone of the Caddy's horn brought Dave to the window. He took one look, making quick eye contact, and dropped the curtains. Glenn stared straight ahead and tapped the steering wheel; thinking of his upcoming date with Ginnie he whispered, "Wild thing! You make my heart sing."

Dave loped across the lawn, patted the Caddy's hood as he rounded the front, and with a fluid motion opened the door and swung into the passenger seat.

"Hey," he said, running his hands through his hair, forcing it back, only to have it fall forward again.

"Hey," Glenn said, "better zip your britches."

"Oh!" Dave said, looking through the gaping opening of his Levi's zipper at his dingy briefs. "Get back in there Little Davy! I'll talk to you later!" He zipped his fly then leaned forward and pulled up his pant leg. From the top of his tube sock he retrieved a bag of weed and a pack of Zig Zag rolling papers. He swept them across Glenn's field of vision with a magician's flare, then stationed them on his lap.

Glenn smiled and said, "Let's go to the west side and get my cousin."

"Cool," Dave said, looking down again. He fumbled for a bud from the baggie, held it to his nose and inhaled, smiling his gummy smile. "Mm, mm," he said, "Dom Perignon, 1934."

He held the bud under Glenn's nose for a sniff of approval. Then he slipped a tissue from the pack and creased it in the fingers of his left hand. He crushed the bud into the fold of fragile paper, and with skill borne of experience rolled the paper around the pot, slid its gummed edge across the tip of his tongue, sealed the joint, twisted the ends, and popped it between his lips.

He straightened his legs, pushed his shoulders against the seat back and shoved his hand deep into his pocket. He came up with an aluminum-wrapped stick of Juicy Fruit and a ticket stub from the Rialto. He tossed the gum onto the dashboard and repeated the process with the other pocket, this time producing lint and a paper clip.

"Damn!" he said, the joint waggling in his mouth. Glenn glanced his way. Dave pushed the button to get into the glove box. Its latch seemed to release, but the door did not fall open. Dave curved his fingers to grasp the top edge of the door and pull, but it would not give way. "Shit!"

"What's the matter?"

"No light!" They rolled to a stop at the intersection of 4th and Mingo Road. A young mother pulled up on their right. When she looked left to check the traffic, she met Dave's smiling wave in the window of the hearse. He gestured to her, rolling his window down. Eyeing the funeral coach, she cranked her window down with a question on her face.

"Hi!" Dave said, holding up the joint. "You wouldn't have a light, would you?"

She rolled her eyes, looked past him to see that the way was clear, and made a right turn away from them.

"I don't think she liked me," Dave said.

Glenn smiled a wry smile, shook his head, and turned left, the unwieldy coach swaying into its lane. They jogged over to 21st Street and headed west. The traffic lights were with them for a while, but each time they encountered a red, Dave tried to make eye contact with another driver.

"This old man's gotta be a smoker!" he said as they eased up next to a battered 1954 Chevrolet pickup, the driver's side window already down. The wizened cowboy behind the wheel wore a plaid shirt and gripped the steering wheel with knobby fingers. The skin of his cheek was blotched red and yellow, his nose gnarly as a leper's. When Dave's gestures caught his peripheral vision, he turned and smacked his lips as he took in first Dave and then the hearse. He shook his head, brought a Styrofoam cup into view, and spit a brown stream into it.

Subdued, Dave ventured nevertheless, "Hey mister? You got a light?" The old man stared a long moment.

Dave shifted in his seat. "We're trying to have a smoke here," he persisted. Without breaking eye contact, the old man let go of the wheel with his right hand, found a matchbook in his shirt pocket, and flipped it as though skipping a stone. It skimmed off the window frame of the hearse and scooted across the dashboard, wedging into the windshield on Glenn's side. Dave watched it in amazement and turned to say thanks, but the cowboy was facing forward. The light turned green; he eased off his clutch and pulled away.

"That was amazing," Dave laughed. "Did you see that? I bet that old man's been skipping stones since the Oklahoma Land Rush!"

Glenn leaned forward, retrieved the matchbook, and handed it to Dave. He pushed the accelerator and the Caddy's engine roared disproportionately to the momentum it attained. They lit the joint with the only match in the book and passed it back and forth as they trundled along past Yale Avenue and Harvard.

Soon enough, the giggles set in. A dog nipped at the air chasing an invisible gnat just as they drove past. Glenn snapped and Dave growled, and for two blocks they laughed. Then, at 7–Eleven a woman's skirt blew up, revealing the seams of her pantyhose and her bare skin beneath.

"Whoa! No panties! Bare pussy, two o'clock!"

Glenn gripped the steering wheel and pulled himself upright, howling. They swerved as he settled back into his seat, pumping the brakes for a red light at Lewis Avenue. The hearse drifted to the right and slowed to a stop, its tires rubbing along the curb. This situation amused them too and they worked the angles on it, wringing out every last gag as they sat at the light and hissed the final few hits from the joint.

"Should we just park here and call it a day?" Glenn tried to hold the smoke in against the laughter throbbing in his midsection.

"Don't move! The curb's holding the air in the tires." Dave spluttered, then snorted; a bubble of snot swelled from his nose. Seeing this, the boys convulsed, arcing their necks back, then curling them forward, as they laughed and gasped for air.

"I'm gonna need some Play-Doh to make that right." Screaming, they doubled over, tears flowing, oblivious to the light turning green and the commuters who'd waited behind them, then swung around and passed them with sidelong glances. They didn't notice the driver who pulled alongside as the light turned yellow and red again.

At last Glenn sat straight, rubbing his face, situating himself behind the wheel. He forced his eyes wide, unaware the light had completed a full cycle and this was his second red. Inhaling deeply, he started to chortle again when a movement to the left caught his eye. Ridiculous in his chauffeur's cap, he turned in time to see Daddy lean across the passenger seat of his 1963 Corvette (the successor to his 1957), his grim face framed as he rolled down the window.

"Oh," Glenn said, "shit."

Dave leaned around to see, then shrank back out of view. "Where'd he come from?"

"He lives a couple of blocks from here. I forgot. He must be going to work."

Glenn told me he sat motionless at first, willing the light to change. But when the light turned green, he glanced again to his left and Daddy signaled for him to pull over. Glenn labored to turn the wheel and the Caddy's tires scrubbed along the curb before they broke free from its concrete grip. He made an immediate right into the parking lot of a dentist's office, stopped and waited.

Again Daddy pulled alongside. He shut off the Corvette's engine and swung out of the car. Swift and graceful, he appeared at the side of the hearse. Glenn stared ahead, took off the chauffeur's cap and handed it to Dave. Daddy waited. At last, Glenn rolled down the hearse's window as though under a spell. Smoke cleared from the cab and flowed upward past Daddy's face, into the morning breeze.

"Why aren't you in school?"

"We're going to West Tulsa," Glenn said, glancing upward.

"No. You're going to turn around and get back to school," Daddy said with hypnotic command.

Glenn rolled the window back up, put the hearse in gear and turned left out of the lot, headed east, toward the school. The Corvette's engine growled back to life and Daddy fell in behind them, a prison guard escorting inmates who complied in silent defeat.

Glenn said Daddy followed them all the way to the school, then did a quick U-turn back toward the freeway and west again, to the refinery.

"He left," Glenn said to Dave. The boys exhaled and shifted in their seats. Glenn maneuvered around the perimeter of the parking lot. He didn't park but pulled up to the drop-off.

From the school entrance, I saw them there talking and shrugged at them, palms up, "What's going on?"

Dave turned to Glenn. "You coming?"

"Naw," Glenn said. "I'll see you later."

"Sorry, man," Dave said. He stuffed the remnants of weed and the pack of rolling papers into Glenn's shirt pocket and got out of the car.

Dave caught up with me and we walked into the building together. Glenn urged the hearse out onto 11th Street and headed east to 129th East Avenue. He drove without conscious thought to the entrance of Floral Haven Cemetery. Keeping his speed low, he lumbered along the curves through the groves of statuary and flat bronze grave markers.

He sat up straight, craning his neck to peer across the Caddy's long hood. Glancing over his shoulder he turned down one unmarked asphalt lane, then another, past a line of saplings staked into the ground and swaying in the sparkling morning sun.

Across from a mausoleum stacked with urns, Glenn pulled the barge onto the grass and pumped the brake until it creaked to a halt.

He threw the lever into park and let his hands drop into his lap. He picked at the skin around his thumbnail as the engine clicked and sighed, letting go of its heat. At last he looked right, toward a square of low hedges enclosing the familiar granite monument with a Masonic compass on its side.

He got out of the hearse and wobbled, his legs numb. Steadying himself, he drew a breath and worked each knee before walking through a break in the hedges toward the monument. He kept his eyes on the ground to his left, counting the bronze markers he passed.

"Here it is," he said to himself. The plaque at his feet was a double. Grandma and Grandpa were buried side-by-side, as though that helped. Tears jumped to his eyes and he squinted them back, looking away across acres of yellowing grass. "Floral Haven," he said, looking down again.

Now he knelt on those graves and began to pull stray shoots of Bermuda grass from around the edges of the marker on Grandpa's side. He paused, sat back on his heels, let his arms hang at his sides.

Then he remembered the pot. Retrieving it from his shirt pocket, he rolled a lumpy joint. He straightened his back, sounded his pockets, and smiled when he came up lighter-free.

He said that's when he saw the groundskeeper. Had he been there all along? The man turned, looked directly at Glenn, and began to walk in his direction. Glenn jerked his chin up and waved. The man in a gray uniform lifted his hand in acknowledgement. Glenn called, "You got a light?"

"Yeah, I might," the man said, close enough now to show thinning blonde hair, bleached eyebrows and glistening stubble. "You got a toke?"

"Yeah," Glenn said, amused, getting to his feet. "Let's get high."

The groundskeeper brought out a yellow Bic, flicked its lever with his grass-stained thumb, and held the flame for Glenn to take the first hit. He drew in the smoke and held it in his lungs, then passed the joint to the man, who took a good hit and held it. "I'll take one more," he said.

"Go ahead, man."

The groundskeeper pulled hard on the joint, burning it down halfway. Holding the smoke in, he handed the joint back, managed a raspy, "Thanks, man," and turned to go.

Glenn watched him for a moment, then looked back toward the hearse, tilted at the edge of the lane. He sat cross-legged facing the bronze marker and pulled idly at the grass around him; a hard-shelled black bug scuttled out of sight. Then he swiveled on his butt and reclined on top of Grandpa. He took the last hit on the joint and flipped it away. Then, lacing his fingers across his belly, he let his muscles relax and he stared up at the cloudless sky.

Chapter Eleven

A Smell in the House

The house on 112th East Avenue where Mom, Glenn, and I lived was the best house among Mom and her siblings, Teetum and Jesse Jr. They acknowledged it outright. Maybe she didn't have enough money to keep it up—teachers' pay was dismal—or maybe the decline in the house mirrored her frame of mind. Maybe, brilliant as she was, she really didn't know any better.

A routine developed of lots and little. Mom brought home bags of groceries after payday. We ate curried chicken, from Majid's recipe. She baked 11x13-inch pans of cinnamon rolls, gooey and sweet, which we gorged on like raptors on the plains, working one gulp after another down the gullet. We had Cokes and ham sandwiches.

As the month wore on, Momma fried hamburgers on the stovetop that we ate with white Rainbow Bread buns from the big bakery on 11th Street, French's yellow mustard, dill pickles and sliced American cheese. Sometimes she made meatloaf. After she paid the phone bill, gas, and electricity on the 15th, we enjoyed Kraft macaroni and cheese for our main meal. Cans of Chef Boyardee Spaghetti-O's and Dinty Moore Beef Stew kept us going up until the first.

In the kitchen, dishes and silverware, pans and utensils, accumulated from breakfast to dinner and breakfast again. Weekend lunches didn't require dishes at the table except maybe a glass for milk. Otherwise, amid scraps and crumbs we picked a spot to settle and ate our baloney and mustard on more Rainbow white bread.

Weekend evenings we might move the dishes to the closest countertop, wipe the table off, and have a game of pinochle with Mom and her girlfriend Zamya.

Finally, when it all got to be too much, Mom would say, "Carolyn, you need to wash the dishes!" And so, standing at the sink where she had washed my hair when I was small enough to lie on my back on the counter with my head dropping back over the rim, I would begin.

Whatever was closest was first into the soapy water, maybe the skillet where she fried the bacon last Saturday with its waxy white topography of congealed grease. Next might come the glasses, each with a hardened ring of milk in the bottom, Mom's most-hated evidence of our carelessness. From fork to saucer, I'd work my way through, stacking each dripping item upon the other in precarious piles that we then whittled down as before.

Out the window above the sink stood the rusty 55-gallon barrel where we burned our household trash. If our cousins were visiting—"the heathens" as Mom called them—we'd race around the flames in the barrel like heathens indeed, screaming and laughing in a near-crazed ritual of childhood release. Once, while tending the fire alone on a blustery autumn afternoon, I pulled one of Mom's discarded sanitary napkins from the flames, not understanding what unfolded in my hands.

No fence separated our yard from our neighbors' yard where a mound of Bermuda grass-covered dirt surrounded the door to their bomb shelter. We three went in once at their invitation—a sort of open house after construction—and huddled with round shoulders in the cool sepulcher, making no eye contact, unclear on proper protocol in that moment, or if there really ever was a bomb.

On the corner of 5th Street and 112th East Avenue, the yard itself was hard-baked Oklahoma clay with fissures an inch wide and tufts of grassy weeds and dandelions. Even in the mornings, our concrete patio radiated heat from the summer day before. Only below the front door did there survive a swath of Bermuda grass, misshapen and incongruous next to the steps and sidewalk. How did our neighbors make it grow?

Before Daddy left, he used to mow the yard with his teeth gritted behind a big Yazoo, its bicycle wheels bumping over the lumpy expanse. Twice he mowed over saplings Mom had started at the corner of the house.

After he moved out, Mom and I huddled together evenings and watched *Lawrence Welk, Red Skelton, Alfred Hitchcock,* and *Perry Mason.* We watched Liberace and Leonard Bernstein weekend mornings, until the TV broke. Then we played Elvis, the Ink Spots, or the Platters on the stereo hi-fi, with pennies taped to the stylus. "Oh yes! I'm

the Great Pretender!" We sang side-by-side, our arms intertwined, our faces lifted. We leaned into each other, our
eyes wide in anticipation of the next track—what would
it be? Oh! That's right! "Smoke Gets in Your Eyes"! And
off we'd go, in the moment, singing and laughing together
when we hit the high notes, so happy, so secure.

***

Mom rented Glenn an E-flat alto sax so he could play in
the school band. Holed up in his room, he practiced the
"Marines' Hymn" day and night. In my bedroom, or the living room, I sang along, "From the halls of Montezoo-ooma
to the shores of Tripoli..." But it was Grandpa's lap steel
guitar that truly inspired him. He bent over it for hours,
tinkering, sussing out melodies, strumming, sliding the
steel along the frets just to hear the sounds he could make.
He never took a lesson. I'm sure he never asked.

By the time Glenn was 16, there was a smell in the house.
It was sweet and stale. Urine. Sweet urine from the night
before. Glenn's room.

Who washed the sheets? He did, I guess. Or Mom did,
eventually. They piled up in the laundry room like the
dishes did in the kitchen, so even when Glenn had fresh
sheets on his bed, the smell hung heavy in the house, cloy-
ing. Maybe his mattress needed airing out, or throwing
away.

If Mom and Glenn discussed the sheets and the mattress,
the smell—the symptoms of the problem—I never knew.
Maybe she talked to Teetum about it, but if she did, she
came away with nothing, a prolonged puzzle, an oddity, a

mystery. Why was he wetting the bed now? Glenn and I didn't talk about it, though I'm sure he would have been mortified by it. And worried.

But we went about our days as though everything was as it had been. As though nothing was wrong. As though there were no piles of heavy sheets in the laundry room. No smell in the house.

God bless Dave. He never talked about the sickly-sweet scent that permeated the atmosphere. Glenn's best friend came day after day, and we all sat in the living room and made nice.

We didn't learn that Glenn's nighttime incontinence was a symptom of juvenile onset diabetes until two years later. At eighteen, he went for a blood test required for a job driving a delivery truck. His blood-sugar level had soared so high that, fearful he was in imminent danger of lapsing into a coma, the shipping company sent him directly to a doctor.

Within the week he brought home tiny needles fitted with syringes he filled with water; he practiced sticking the needles through the rind of an orange and plunging the water into the pulp. Vials of insulin cooled in the fridge. The vials had fixed rubber membranes clamped on their tops, and soon Glenn looked like Dr. Kildare, inserting a needle through the membrane, tipping the vial upside down, drawing back the plunger and measuring out insulin. He thumped the syringe like a pro and pushed out a bubble. Then he stuck himself.

"Ow!" he cried, ever dramatic.

"Does it hurt?" I asked the obvious.

"Hell yes, it hurts! I'm sticking myself with a needle! Here, you want some?" He swung the needle toward me and I dodged.

Not long after the injections began, the bedwetting stopped. No more smell. No more dank dampness. His room and his problem dried up. An anomaly soon set aside.

I don't think Momma even knew that diabetes runs in families. I never heard her talk about it, nor Teetum. Grandma was dead by then. How could Momma know?

Chapter Twelve

Haircut

Most likely, Glenn came to the attention of East Central High School's football team by way of a cheerleader, Angie Marshall. The girls all thought he was cute. He was cute. And funny. Wry, like Grandpa had been. Self-deprecating. Perfect. Appealing.

Another advantage was his hair. In 1967 you couldn't do much better than having Beatles' hair, and Glenn had it. His fine, silky-brown hair grew out perfectly into a Paul McCartney mop. Glenn knew it looked good. He developed a tick of throwing his head to the right, his hair swinging and settling just so. It didn't go unnoticed.

He cultivated his natural advantage of being funny. He could flirt by making the girls laugh and they loved being around him. He treated them well. His thoughtful attention made the girls feel good.

He dressed well, too, in those days, pre-hippy. His white cords and spray-starched button-down shirts gave him a preppy overtone, well-kept, but, with the hair, edgy.

He had his own girlfriend, Patti Lee. Wholesome and scholarly. Pretty and plain all at once. Out of the spotlight. Low key. Loving. I'd be surprised if Angie's boyfriend, Butch Clark, took much notice of Glenn and Angie before she started talking.

Yep, I'll bet it was Angie that made Butch draw a bead on Glenn. She must have repeated a story where Glenn was the star. Maybe it was from biology, when Glenn drank that cup of apple juice in front of the class after they had been directed to bring urine samples in baby food jars. She probably pointed Glenn out in the hallways. Only five foot, seven inches, after all, he was well below their normal plane of vision.

It doesn't matter now, of course. Whatever the reason, the fact is that the offensive line, those big, corn-fed, crew-cut sides of beef, began to focus on Glenn. Butch Clark was at the front of the line. A true cowboy, most days Butch wore a black felt cowboy hat over his buzz-cut black hair with white scalp showing through. His hairline had a natural point to it. The bristly black widow's peak accentuated his pointed chin, his straight eyebrows slanting toward his pointed nose, and his dark, pupilless eyes.

Butch acted as apex of the wedge, bow-legged and swaggering in the parking lot, the hallways, and the cafeteria. With him always were his minions, just at his shoulders, fawning, obsequious, listening for a thought, a directive, a signal: Dirk Brown, Jack Norman, Tommy Curtis, and Robby Johnson.

The five of them wore their jerseys on game days and bruised their way through doorways and to the front of the lunch line with the careless arrogance of the entitled. They took food off underlings' trays, forced them out of seats they fancied, and made contact with elbows and shoulders whenever it suited them. They laughed loud with their mouths full, showing half-chewed chunks of yeast rolls and schoolhouse lasagna. They ate with curved backs and forearms on the tables. They left their trays and trash for the custodians to clear away.

"Now," thought Butch, "who is this little brown-haired squib? More importantly, why is my girlfriend talking about him?"

Robby spotted Glenn first, leaving school in his oxidized maroon 1949 Ford, with Patti Lee sitting on the bench seat next to him.

"Hey, Clark, there's the little smartass." Butch turned and squinted.

"That's him, huh? He don't look like much."

"Nah," said Robby, "he ain't much at all."

They piled into Butch's 1958 Chevy pickup, each side squeaking and sagging to accommodate their bulk. Butch turned the key and the truck rumbled to a start. Clutch in, he jostled and waggled the gear shifter on the steering column until it dropped into first. As they rolled toward the exit, Jack, Dirk and Tommy loped alongside and vaulted into the truck bed.

"Yee haw! Giddy up! Git along little doggie!" They pounded the glass of the cab's back window and the sides of the truck bed with meaty fists. Butch pumped the clutch and jammed the gas pedal, jerking the truck into screeching its tires. The three in the back fell over each other laughing and they careened out of the lot onto 11th Street.

They caught up to Glenn and Patti Lee at the intersection of 11th and Garnett. Pulling up on their right, Butch revved the truck's engine until Patti Lee turned her head. On eye contact, Butch raised his pelvis into view and thrust his tongue out to a point, wagging it as he rubbed his crotch. When Glenn leaned around to see past Patti Lee, Butch dropped back into the seat, turned his head away, popped the clutch, and lurched through the intersection, his passengers screaming with white faces and red ears.

Glenn and Patti Lee looked at each other and spoke in unison, "Jerks."

The weekend went by without a flutter. ECHS beat Will Rogers 24 to 20. The defensive line made some key tackles, breaking through the Ropers' offense, cracking an opponent's ribs, and twisting another's knee in the dog pile. In the locker room after the game, they drank vodka. Later, parked in her driveway next to her daddy's Chevrolet Impala, Butch hoisted Angie's cheerleading skirt and scraped her thigh with his zipper.

Glenn and Patti Lee went to see *Cool Hand Luke* at the Rialto downtown. They ate a cupcake and drank sloe gin fizzes to celebrate their six-month anniversary and made love in the back seat of the Ford. They stood on her front porch under the yellow light and kissed tender kisses before she went inside. Glenn drove the three blocks home, let himself in, and slept on top of the covers, fully clothed.

Monday in Biology, Angie smiled at Glenn. When he waved back, Mr. Eisner saw him.

"Simpson, what's on your mind?"

"Nothing."

"Oh, it must be something, Simpson. You aren't waving to Miss Marshall for nothing."

"Good looks, then," Glenn said, glancing toward Angie. She smiled another quick smile before looking back at Mr. E, devoid of expression.

"Good looks it is! And a fine choice too, though probably out of your league."

Glenn looked down with a squint, pressing his lips together with the slightest shake of his head.

"Anything else, Simpson?" Glenn gave silent, steady eye contact. "Like number seventeen from the worksheet. That is where we were before Mr. Simpson took us afield, isn't it? What did you put down for number seventeen, Mr. Simpson?"

"Amoeba."

"Hooray! Mr. Simpson got one right! Mark your calendars ladies and gentlemen and let's move on. Number eighteen. Who can tell me the secret of number eighteen?"

A buzzing arose in Glenn's brain as he watched Mr. Eisner pace back and forth across the front of the room, calling numbers and names. Soon he began thinking of his car, of Patti Lee. Through louder buzzing he watched the second hand on the clock above the door sweep past the twelve, and the minute hand tick toward the two. One minute till the bell.

Glenn pushed his worksheet to the edge of the lab table and closed his biology book. He plopped the book on top of his blue cloth-covered binder, drawing Mr. Eisner's attention again.

"What is it now, Simpson?"

Glenn stood up and his worksheet slipped to the floor. He pushed his chair under the table, took his book and binder and walked toward the door.

"Simpson!"

The buzzing in Glenn's brain matched the buzzing of the bell as he crossed the threshold into the shiny bright hallway. Students from other classrooms spilled into the thoroughfare.

"Simpson!"

Glenn kept walking as a thrill worked up his back and into his scalp. Mr. Eisner reached the doorway then moved aside as the rest of his class turned past him on their way to lunch. Angie Marshall led the way.

"Glenn!" she called, but Glenn didn't answer. All he wanted was out.

***

The days leading up to Homecoming hummed, the drone tensing to a higher pitch with each event calculated to build school spirit.

Butcher paper banners taped across the cafeteria's entrance heralded the dance, themed "Surfin' USA." The Student Leadership class spent its evenings and weekends building props for the dance with giant waves fashioned out of plywood, cardboard, blue and white tempera paint, and tissue paper. Female mannequins on loan from JC

Penney modeled bikinis and ponytails. The males sported Hawaiian swim trunks, huaraches, and dark glasses. They would soon dance a static dance to the Beach Boys' harmonies streaming from a cassette player, burrowed into sand unloaded by the City of Tulsa Parks & Recreation Department.

The day of the homecoming game, an all-school rally was set up in the gym. The bleachers were down and students from every wing of the school poured into their respective sections, their excitement echoing off the lacquered floors and cinder block walls. Freshmen here, sophomores here, juniors here. And graduating seniors in the section of honor.

Red and white helium balloons lined the banisters. Crepe paper streamers twisted to show alternating red and white draped from the center of the ceiling to the corners of the gym. The marching band thumped out the school's song as the drum major, with arched back and baton pumping, led the color guard to the center of the floor. "Give a song, give a yell, give a cheer! We will stand for East Central forever!"

On cue, senior football players and cheerleaders filed into the VIP seats on the floor in front of the senior section. Butch Clark and his cronies took front row seats. Just then, Glenn came along the front of the bleachers. He hadn't been in classes that morning but wanted to sit with Patti Lee for the rally. His eyes were up in the stands, searching for her as he made his way across the front of the VIP seats.

Again, Robby spotted him first. He elbowed Butch and jerked his head in Glenn's direction. Butch's black eyes locked onto Glenn, assessing him, his confidence growing. This would be easy.

As Glenn came parallel to Butch, Butch pushed his cowboy boot out, grazing Glenn's ankle. When Glenn turned and made eye contact, Butch made a mocking lunge in his direction. Glenn side-stepped and frowned at Butch. He then affected the tic that sent his hair swinging to the right, the gesture a dismissal. Just then Patti Lee caught his eye and he smiled up at her, waving as he turned up the aisle in her direction.

"I'm going to get that little shit," Butch said to Robby.

"Huh? Oh yeah. We'll get him."

***

"Imagine me and you. I do. / I think about you day and night. It's only right..." Homecoming couples sang along and danced to the Turtles' upbeat tune, until Butch and Angie's argument escalated in tone and volume. She shouted. He maintained a guttural monotone. Something about who owned who or who was boss. She in her bare feet and he with a grip on her bicep. Just at the edge of hearing, a long, low growl of thunder rumbled across Tulsa. A silent flash of lightning preceded a crack of electricity and the opening of the sky as Butch steered Angie off the dance floor and to their table; the other couples parted, opened a lane, well-trained as they were to accommodate these two high-profile actors.

Butch held tight and pushed her forward so that, in an almost graceful flourish, she swooped down and snagged her shoes, silver sling-backs; he pocketed his flask. Then, in one fluid motion, he strode toward the exit, never loosening his grip or unclenching his jaw; she tripped alongside on her toes. She had lowered her voice but snarled without pause until the metal door clacked shut behind them and, through the frosted glass, their silhouettes receded.

Perhaps Angie felt embarrassed, or Butch enraged, by their public display. More likely, any associated emotions made up a familiar repertoire they played out in a personal theater with an audience of two. Nobody else cared. By the time the next song started, "The Beat Goes On," with Sonny & Cher and a strong bass line, Butch and Angie's wake had closed and the other attendees returned to their own urgencies. For Glenn and Patti Lee, this meant twisting away and slow dancing and drifting out the door just ahead of the crowd. They paused beside Dave and Francie before dashing into the parking lot. In that brief moment, the boys exchanged a nod and one word, "Cotton's."

Indeed, their Saturday night unfolded like most others for the two young lovers; Glenn's jacket and Patti Lee's party dress came off and went back on with little difficulty, and the late night after-party started for the boys.

Once the girls were in their respective homes, Glenn and Dave met at Cotton's, Tulsa's venerable pool hall. A reclaimed storefront in a strip center with blacked-out windows, grimy carpet, and smoggy air, Cotton's sported 15 pool tables, foosball, ping-pong, darts, and a perimeter of pinball machines, all populated by tired men in saggy britches with thick hair, squinty eyes, and stacks of quarters on the side.

Glenn and Dave smoked cigarettes, laying them on the corner of the table when they chalked their cue sticks. They moved around the table like bullfighters, graceful and calculating. With perfect geometry they leaned across the green felt, slid their sticks, and watched the hard, heavy, resin balls disperse around the pockets, the cue ball returning to its pre-designated spot each time, according to English.

Gordon dashed in from the rain shaking his fatigue jacket and carrying a brown paper bag. So they set up a rotation to include him, odd man playing the winner. But Gordon wasn't very good, so the game came back to Glenn and Dave, Dave and Glenn.

Gordon had two pints of Wild Turkey and three bottles of Coke in the bag at his feet. They took turns with that as well. Cotton didn't pay much attention to them, or anyone else. He mostly smoked and watched the old-timers knock balls around the table closest to him and the cash register.

By two o'clock, Glenn, Dave and Gordon had exhausted the bourbon and Coke, the Pall Malls, and their supply of quarters. They ducked their heads, ran across the parking lot, and sat in Glenn's Ford to smoke one joint, and then another.

They laughed about the rotation and Gordon's miserable lack of skill with a cue stick. They laughed about Ed Sullivan's posture, and made lewd jokes about Topo Gigio, and Señor Wences. They talked with reverence about Vietnam, their birthdates, and Gordon's flat feet.

At last they fell silent and let their butts slip down in the seats, their heads resting on the seat backs. Each one drifted. Maybe they slept. The rain stopped and the clouds parted, showing a Harvest Moon and sparkling stars between the remaining tufts of clouds passing overhead. After a time, Dave stirred, and when he did, Gordon came alive too.

"I guess I'll go," Dave said, opening the door without ceremony.

Gordon exited with only a perfunctory, "See ya."

Slouched behind the wheel, Glenn watched as they each slid into their own cars, started up and eased onto 11th Street toward the Wagon Wheel addition, Dave to his parents' house and Gordon to his grandma's.

Only then did Glenn straighten himself into an upright position, take the steering wheel, and turn the key in the ignition. The Ford started up and KAKC blared. Glenn grabbed the volume knob and turned it left until he realized it was Jim Morrison. He cranked it back to the right as he rolled onto the deserted thoroughfare, wet from the downpour. "Come on, baby, light my fire!"

Bleary-eyed and singing loud, Glenn rolled along next to the curb. At first he didn't notice the pick-up and El Camino on the street behind him. Butch and his crew were still three blocks back and didn't see Glenn either. They were playing at drag racing. Side by side, they floored the gas and popped their clutches, made their tires spin, squealing along, and starting over at each new intersection.

Poised at the last corner behind Glenn, Jack held the wheel of the El Camino with his left hand, gestured toward Glenn's Ford with a can of Coors in his right, and called across to Butch, "Hey, there's your buddy!"

Butch's head swiveled a sloppy loop; he willed it to steady. In a moment, his black eyes focused and then his brain seized the circumstance.

"Let's get that son of a bitch!" he said. Again, he popped his clutch and the truck's tires spun. Jack floored the El

Camino and it fishtailed on the wet pavement. Butch roared up behind Glenn honking and flashing his headlights.

Glenn looked up and winced from the stab of light in his rearview mirror. Jack pulled up beside him and, reflexively, Glenn hit his brakes. Jack then veered right cutting off Glenn's escape. Butch slammed on his brakes and killed the truck's engine. He threw open the glove box in front of Robby. Four pairs of scissors clattered onto the floorboard.

"Where'd you get this shit?" Robby said, gathering the shears with both hands.

"Every teacher has a pair," Butch grinned. "Come on!"

Jack and Dirk, already out of the El Camino, jerked Glenn's door open; it never would lock. Suddenly sober, Glenn leaned across toward the passenger side, but Robby was there. He lunged at Glenn, shoved him into the grasp of the offensive linesmen who jerked him out of the Ford and threw him to the wet pavement.

Glenn thrashed against them, kicked the underside of his own car, bruised his shins, and felt his pants soak through from the pooled water on the asphalt. Jack and Dirk tightened their grips, each now with a one-armed half nelson, and wrenched Glenn's arms behind his back.

Robby came around, stepped across Glenn's legs and sat on his knees. "Hold still, little man," he said leaning into Glenn's face. "Look what I've got!" He displayed the scissors and Glenn twisted away, grunting in horror.

Then Butch stepped into view. "Here," he said looking down, holding out his hand for a weapon. Robby handed him Miss Briscoe's blue-handled shears from the art room. Butch opened the shears wide, exposing the sharp inner

edges of the blades, and handed them to Jack. "Make sure
he holds still."

Jack took the shears with his free hand and held the point
next to Glenn's left eye. Dirk grabbed the crown of Glenn's
hair, his fine, shiny, Paul McCartney hair, and, with a hard
twist, Glenn was immobilized, his eyes bulging, reeling in
their sockets, straining to see where the first blow would
come from.

It came from Butch, but it wasn't a blow. Butch squatted
on his haunches and took a black-handled pair of scissors.
"Here now," he said looking at Glenn with a snake's smile,
"I've wanted to do this for a long time." He took a clump of
Glenn's bangs and hacked at it, sawed at it until it came off
in his hand. He chuckled and showed it to Glenn. Glenn
screamed through clenched teeth, tears springing to his
eyes.

"Oh, now, don't cry! This won't take long." Butch tossed
Glenn's hair aside then took another clump and another,
twisting them into ropes and grinding the blades against
their bulk.

Robby pulled a patch from Glenn's temple so hard
that his skin came to a peak underneath, and Mrs.
Holder's scissors snipped it, leaving a bloody gouge.
Glenn shrieked. "Aw, I'm sorry man, did that hurt?"
Robby said. He wiped the blade on his pant leg and
reached for more.

Butch and Robby worked methodically around Glenn's
skull. Jack and Dirk moved in concert, stepping over Butch
and around Robby, forcing Glenn to offer the back of his
head.

At last, Butch rocked back on his heels; Robby stood up with a groan and leaned against the Ford's open door. "There you go!" said Butch, patting Glenn's cheek. Glenn never averted his blazing eyes. "Fuck you," he said.

Butch chuckled again and stood. Jack and Dirk relinquished their hold, and Glenn sank for a moment before he bent his knees and came up on his elbows. With that, Butch kicked Glenn's side with the pointed toe of his boot, for an instant spreading his ribs. Then Robby kicked his nuts. Glenn rolled to his left and began to retch.

"Let's go," Butch said, and turned back to his truck.

Dirk gave one last kick, a glancing blow to Glenn's tufted, bleeding head. Then he got into the El Camino. Jack floored it, popped the clutch, and spun gravel onto Glenn's curved body.

Butch and Robby rolled by slowly and Robby spit out the passenger side window, but it missed. "Aw shit," he said. "Let's go."

And they did.

***

My dad came to the house after that and heard the story as we sat in the living room, where I'd heard him argue with my mom so long before. Glenn already had a buzz cut by then, so his hair was more or less uniform over his head. He had scabs at odd places, mostly on Robby's side, the skin around the gouges crusty and inflamed.

Daddy got up and took his formidable presence to the school, but nothing happened there. It was the weekend, after all. Off school grounds. If the police got involved, we never heard of it.

Butch and his crew drove by the house one afternoon and slowed long enough for an exchange of insults and vulgarities but moved on.

I don't know if any revenge was ever exacted, though I wouldn't put it past my dad. All I know is that Glenn never went back to that school. I guess he'd learned enough.

Chapter Thirteen

Jim Lyons & the Shotgun

It took years for me to piece together the parallel worlds of my parents. When my dad drove away from the house with his work shirts in the Corvette and tears in his eyes, I, like a dull-witted neighbor, had an ill-formed thought about an argument between them that kept me up one night. An amorphous question floated at the periphery, low to the ground, like smoke from an untended bed of coals, a dwindling campfire just in the woods there, beyond the range of my comprehension.

I remember Mom told me once that the best place to hide things from Daddy was in her Kotex box. "He will never look in there," she said. A silverfish of confusion slipped through the seam of my consciousness—what would she be hiding from Daddy? Why must she hide things from him?—and wriggled itself away into the files marked "Re-open When It's Too Late to Ask" and "Do Not Open Until Your Own Marriage is Falling Apart and Everyone Who

Knows Anything About This Kind of Stuff is Dead." Yeah, good idea, keep it there.

When my daddy stared at that carhop's ass, or picked up a woman from the corner once when I was staying the weekend with him, those stray scraps of information went into the shoebox of my ill-equipped mind, only to produce wonder or forehead slaps later, much later.

So, maybe Mom dated after she and Daddy split. Maybe she was even open about it, but I don't think so. I only knew she went to work teaching math at Nathan Hale High School on the other side of town. Glenn and I went to school close to the house and had the place to ourselves in the afternoons before she could get home from her school to supervise. We lived our lives, she lived hers; I guess Daddy lived his life too.

But Jim Lyons's arrival mandated adjustments across all fronts.

Jim taught shop at my mom's school. No doubt they met there. But the appeal? The attraction? I still don't get it. I don't remember seeing them courting, or any breaking-in period. I don't remember Mom introducing us, though surely she did. All I know for certain is they got married. He moved in with us. It didn't go well.

I was gangly and hesitant then. Thirteen years old. Compliant. I wanted everyone to be happy and to like me. That's how it was with Jim. I had questions about him—"Where did he come from?" or, "What's he doing here?"—but they remained formless, like Jim himself—vague; non-committal. And Mom seemed energized, happy. So, I never asked. Mostly I wanted peace in the house.

I had been flustered when kids at school asked why my mom's last name was different from mine. I felt confused, embarrassed for not knowing. I didn't know why Jim was there or how to explain anything. An enormous flood of relief washed through me when one day after school I happened to be standing near Becky McNamara, THE cutest, most popular girl in the seventh grade, and someone asked her why her mom's name was different from hers. Becky shrugged and said casually, "She got remarried."

"That's it! That's what I'll say! Hallelujah! My mom got remarried!

Glenn, on the other hand, was suspicious of Jim from the start. But his interactions with Jim were neither dismissive nor open, rather, ostensibly neutral. Glenn observed this new arrival as a scientist would, holding in reserve his assessment of a specimen in a petri dish.

That changed the instant Jim called Glenn an oddball.

They were looking at a group picture of us and all our cousins. It must have been taken at Easter a couple of years before. All eleven of us were lined up in Grandma's front yard, squinting into the sun. The other boys wore Wrangler's jeans and buzz-cut hair. Jesse's boys looked like the 4-H kids they were, muscular, tan. Teetum's boys were awkward, smiling goofy smiles, T-shirts askew. And Glenn, already tuned into the British Invasion, looked it, with his over-the-ears, mop-cut hair brushed forward, long-sleeved white shirt with oversized pointed collars and a paisley brocade vest.

"You just don't fit in, buddy." Jim tapped Glenn's face in the snapshot and chuckled in the deliberate, cynical manner we'd already come to expect. He seemed gleeful to point out the difference. Of all the things to quip about, he'd stumbled on the one that pierced Glenn's confidence—his uncertainty about belonging in the family. Glenn pulled away, flushed with anger, and said, "Fuck you."

He stood to leave, and Jim laughed again and called after him, "It's just a joke. What're you so mad about?" Jim turned to look at Mom with feigned innocence. "What did I do?"

After that, Glenn didn't care about peace. He made no effort to disguise his distaste for our new stepdad.

Jim was more guarded, too. He didn't make any more overt comments about Glenn, and his eyes always followed Glenn in the room. He might have to tilt the top edge of the newspaper down to see Glenn move from the hallway across the corner of the living room, through the dining room and into the kitchen.

Always wary. Glenn made no eye contact. Why would he look at a worm on the sidewalk?

Meals became strategic undertakings with timing, placement, and word choice tactical imperatives. If Jim spoke, let's say at dinnertime, to voice how he preferred his hamburger, Glenn would snort at his choice. And whatever Jim's choice was, Glenn would choose the opposite.

Jim did not try to raise us, or to participate in our lives. He seemed an observer, a bemused critic. He might comment on my new school clothes, but never on Glenn's comings and goings. The last time he asked Glenn where he was going, Glenn said he was going to get drunk and fuck a sheep.

By contrast, Jim seemed to find me diverting. Each summer I put my visionary nature and organizational skills to work casting neighborhood kids in talent shows. Once, under my direction, half a dozen of us performed "Blue Hawaii" in the living room for Mom and Jim. I taped a penny to the arm of the hi-fi and carefully dropped the needle on the space leading to the correct band of Elvis's album. My friends and I sang along: "Night and you, and blue Hawa-a-a-ii." We did an awkward hula and swayed our arms side-to-side, imagining ocean breezes and a twinkle in the eye of The King. Jim laughed and clapped, asking, "Who did the choreography?" I felt unsure since I didn't know the word. But Mom looked happy too, and nodded, so I said, "I did."

More than once, Jim hurt my mom's feelings. This night, she was changing clothes and changing clothes, getting ready to go back to school for a PTA meeting. Jim and I were at the kitchen table, he with the ever-present newspaper; I picked at a pork chop.

Mom came in wearing her third outfit, a skirt and sweater. She had gained weight and the skirt was tight. "How's this?" she asked, clearly miserable with rounded belly and rounded butt.

"Is your skirt supposed to cup under like that?" Jim said, with his hand forming said cup and scooping to show what he saw.

Mom sputtered and tears came to her eyes. She tugged at the sweater as she rushed from the room, grazing the doorjamb as she went. Jim went back to his newspaper, and I could hear mom thrashing about in her bedroom. She left out the other door, through the living room, closing the front door firmly and letting the screen door slam.

I kept my head down as she started her '57 Mercury Turnpike Cruiser—the one my dad bought her after we came home from Abadan—and backed out of the driveway. When she pulled away from the house, Jim folded the newspaper and carried it with him to the living room and sat down. The TV still didn't work. Even with him there we couldn't afford to get it fixed. He re-opened the paper and started over.

They argued when she came home that night, Mom and Jim. I could hear their voices, his measured and infuriating. Mom's clipped and sarcastic. Glenn probably heard them too; his room was just across the hall.

By now Glenn was sixteen and plenty angry. He stayed gone most of the time. I remember one time, when he came through the house to get something from his room, Jim said, "Well! Look who dropped by! Look what the cat dragged in!"

Glenn, walking swiftly, barely turned his head as he lifted the middle finger of his left hand. Moments later, he came back through the room in the opposite direction with his pale-yellow windbreaker over his arm. This time, he showed the middle finger of his right hand. Jim sniffed and shook his head, chuckling to himself.

Outside, Glenn jumped into the passenger seat of Dave's Oldsmobile. I could only hear the last word in his sentence when they lurched backwards out of the driveway—"asshole." Dropping the Olds into drive, Dave managed to squeal the tires. The big sedan sank low in back and rose in front as they roared down 112th East Avenue, each boy with an elbow on his respective window frame.

By now, Jim had been in the house two years. He taught woodshop and came home at 4:15 every afternoon in a short-sleeved plaid shirt and Lee jeans. No lesson plans, no papers to grade. He settled in the same corner of the couch where my daddy used to sit and waited for my mom and dinner.

Before he moved in, the toilet seat in our bathroom wobbled and slipped to the side when you sat. It still did. The frame of the window over the kitchen sink had rotted after years of north wind and rain. Now the wind whistled through the porous corner of the spongy wood that stayed in place if you forced the glass upward to let in a breeze. The door from the kitchen into the garage hung askew on hinges with stripped screws. We developed a technique of "lift and close" to get it back in place if we opened it. And the screen to the back door leaned against the side of the house before Jim Lyons appeared. It also failed to catch the wood-shop teacher's attention.

I don't know if Jim gave my mom any money. I do know we didn't eat any better after he moved in. Maybe more regularly. He had his expectations for meals by the clock.

Then they began to argue. Mom told me years later, after we learned Jim died of a brain tumor, that he had changed suddenly during their short marriage. His personality changed, she said. According to her, he went from good guy to bad guy in pretty short order. She thought the tumor explained it. I had no recollection of the good guy.

Glenn wouldn't have described a change in Jim. He saw Jim as an interloper, a pretender, an offending detractor with an arrogant smirk.

Each taunted the other. Glenn, with the unreasonable certainty only a teenager can muster. Jim, with the foolish arrogance of a poker player drawing on an inside straight. They picked at each other, each taking delight in the acrimonious game.

Of a morning, we could find Jim at the kitchen table in his jeans and plaid shirt, his thinning hair brushed straight back from his face. It had receded on the sides of his forehead, leaving a strip down the center of longer strands Brylcreemed into stasis.

His forearm rested next to his cereal bowl, spoon poised for the next scoop. He waited Glenn out, smiling to himself when Glenn paced into the room. When Glenn chose not to eat rather than share the space, Jim counted that as a victory.

Glenn spit on the windshield of Jim's truck every morning when he left for school, savoring the effort and the effect. It pleased him most when a gooey glob landed just at driver's eye level.

Day after day, the struggle went on. Momma seemed to understand Glenn's point of view but didn't try to intervene or explain one to the other. After all, Jim hadn't risen to the pre-game hype. Maybe she rationalized that things would smooth over, or that Glenn would move out soon enough. Maybe she just didn't know what to do.

But Glenn was formulating an idea.

On a Sunday afternoon Mom and I went to Skiatook to visit her best friend Zamya. While we were gone, Glenn said, he emerged from a long sleep and headed for the kitchen. But Jim was there ahead of him, standing and staring into our dingy, round-shouldered fridge. He leaned over and pushed aside the baloney in hopes of finding some of last night's meatloaf. He glanced to the side to find Glenn there, in line for something to eat.

He turned back to the fridge and began to whistle as he elongated his search. Maybe he'd need some grape jelly. No. What's this in the aluminum foil? Oh, it's that goulash with the crusty edge. Nope.

"Make up your mind and get out of my way," Glenn said.

Jim straightened up in the wedge of space made by the open door of the fridge. He smiled that infuriating smile and flinched at Glenn, a full body surge, making Glenn step back.

"I'll kill you, you stupid son of a bitch," Glenn said, as he turned away and headed back to his bedroom.

Jim laughed a little laugh, put a bowl of potato salad under his left arm and rested the baloney on the Saran Wrap stretched across the top. He balanced the mustard there, grabbed a head of iceberg lettuce, and swiveled toward the table; he bent his knee and shut the refrigerator door with his upturned heel.

I don't remember if Glenn said where he got the gun. Maybe it had been Grandpa's. I didn't know he had it—a shotgun with two long barrels side-by-side. It must have been in his closet or under his bed a long time. It was old-looking and heavy. He was unaccustomed to wielding it. He paused outside his bedroom door and swung it awkwardly up to his shoulder.

He walked down the hall and crossed the living room with the gun swaying. When he rounded the corner in the dining room and Jim came into view, he stopped and stabilized himself, spread his feet, put his cheek on the cool dry wood of the gun's stock and his finger on the trigger.

Jim sat as usual, back curved over his food: baloney, white bread, and yellow mustard. The potato salad sat with its weepy Saran Wrap skin peeled back. Jim held it hostage, his fork hovering.

He felt Glenn's presence more than he saw anything from his peripheral view. But he sat chewing like a cow, looking ahead, across the kitchen at…what? Crumbs on the countertops? Yesterday's breakfast dishes with egg yolks hardening? That north window he could have repaired? Rude and defiant, he took another bite of his sandwich and poked at the potato salad with his fork.

Glenn stood still and took shallow breaths, not noticing the weight of the gun now. No hurry.

Jim snorted and smiled to himself and turned at last to see Glenn and the gun leveled at him.

His smirk fell and his features went round and wide; eyes, mouth, and nostrils now circles in stretched white skin. He wanted to say something, but no words came. He dropped the fork and pushed his chair back with the calves of his legs as he rose. The chair teetered and tipped backwards, its back bumped against the wall.

"Good," Glenn said. "Get up and go, you prick." Jim moved his butt across the edge of the table, not wanting to get any closer to Glenn or to lose sight of him. He took a sidestep toward the door that led from the kitchen through the laundry room and into our mom's bedroom.

Glenn took two steps forward, kept his cheek on the smooth wood; his left eye squinted, his right eye followed Jim through the gun's metal notch of a sight at the end of the double barrels.

"Wait," Jim said. He tried to get out of the room, bumbled and felt his way so as not to turn his head.

"No," Glenn said. "No more waiting. You gotta go, you fucking prick piece of shit."

Jim broke for the door, crashed through it, and slammed the door to the bedroom behind him.

Glenn stepped quickly. Never intending to open the door, he smashed the gun against it again and again for maximum clatter.

"Hurry up asshole!"

Jim flew across the bedroom, through the other door and into the hallway, out the front door and into his truck. Glenn leapt through the house, stepped onto the front porch and again brought the gun to his shoulder. He aimed it at the truck's windshield and smiled at the dried spot of spit he'd left there the night before.

Jim cranked up the truck, threw it into reverse, lurched backwards across the yard and over the curb onto 112th East Avenue. Glenn took two more steps forward as Jim wrestled the truck into first gear, popped the clutch, and, looking back over his shoulder, raced to the end of the block.

Glenn allowed the gun's barrel to drop and stood there in the sun for a good long while. He enjoyed deep breaths and thought of nothing in particular. Then he went in, sat on the couch, and waited for Mom and me to come home.

I don't remember seeing Jim after that, though he surely returned to gather his belongings. They divorced without incident; after all, there was little investment on either side. I looked for an effect on Mom, but none was perceptible. If she cried, or they hashed things out over the phone, I never knew. It was almost a non-event. The lost chapter of my mom's second husband. That stone created few ripples in this pond. Or so it seemed.

Like my daddy, Jim was wrapped up, taped into a box, and gone.

The three of us, Mom, Glenn, and I, reverted to our routines. We only talked about Jim that one time when we came home and Glenn told us the story. Mom only said, "Oh," and "Oh," again. She didn't evince surprise or anger. She didn't wonder—not aloud anyway—where Jim went or if he would come back. Maybe she was in shock. Maybe she was relieved. If she'd been trying to figure out how to undo what she'd done by marrying Jim, that riddle had been solved with Glenn's direct approach.

Indeed, only Glenn seemed clear, as though he'd had a plan, carried it out, and anticipated the outcome. "Here," he said and showed us the rusty gun with its bent hammer. It wasn't loaded, and couldn't have fired if it had been.

That was a good thing.

Chapter Fourteen

The Other End
of the Spectrum

Mom said, "I've taken a job in Arizona."

That's how Glenn and I learned what she'd been think-ing. She presented her decision—a fait accompli. She had thought it through, researched the job market, applied, in-terviewed, and accepted a position without our detecting any shift in the atmosphere.

If she gave a rationale that day, it made no impression. Years later, when George Strait sang, "All My Exes Live in Texas," I said to myself, that must have been it. "Texas is a place I'd dearly love to be / But all my exes live in Texas / And that's why I hang my hat in Tennessee."

Maybe she needed to put a little distance. Although she had only two exes—my dad and Jim Lyons—that might have been impetus enough, though I couldn't see why. After the shotgun, we never saw or heard from Jim; my dad and she never talked, either, as far as I could see, save for the perfunctory arranging of his weekend visits with me. Clearly though, in retrospect, I didn't see much at all of what her life was like apart from Glenn and me. I saw only what related to us. She had more than that on her mind—no doubt.

After she died, I found letters she had saved from Jake Leonard. He was also a math teacher. They met at Horace Mann Junior High School in Tulsa. He moved from Oklahoma to Arizona at some point along the line and they kept in touch. She missed him. That, too, had escaped my notice. I think she loved Jake, or at least she was infatuated. In lust, perhaps.

An unfortunate consequence of dying without advance planning is that your children will read your personal mail. Within days of Mom's stroke, I came to appreciate her as a fully-fledged human being. Jake Leonard's randy letters left no questions unanswered. After that, if I held onto any ignorance, or innocence, it was dispelled the afternoon in Williams when we were emptying her house and I found a dildo tucked into her sock drawer.

My guess is that she tried to find a job in Phoenix, where Jake lived, but it was not to be. She took a job at Williams High School in Williams, Arizona. Gateway to the Grand Canyon. Route 66. She rented from the town's undertaker, a thin, bent, colorless man she described as "too helpful." It snowed 90 inches the first winter she lived there, blocking all exits from her house. To free her, the undertaker dug a tunnel to her front door and knocked. When she opened the door to find him standing in the hollow, sweating, shovel in hand, she threw her arms around him in a desperate hug.

That fall, the undertaker's son was killed in Vietnam. A sealed casket delivered to his very own place of business left him undone. He told Mom his grief overwhelmed him. No other thought could penetrate the veil. He had to see his son one more time. So he worked through the night with an acetylene torch from his days as a Navy welder and cracked the casket's seal. When he opened the container, it was empty save for a couple of sandbags; he guessed they were there for the weight.

Right away, Mom distinguished herself among staff and students at Williams HS. Her picture appeared on multiple pages of the yearbook; notes from her students cluttered the margins, expressing their appreciation for her brilliance, her wit, and her powerful teaching style—as irresistible in Arizona as they had been in Tulsa. "You're the BEST, Mrs. Lyons!" "I never would have gotten quadratic triangles without you!" And, "To the coolest teacher I know—thanks for everything—even the math."

Immediately upon her declaration of intent to move to Arizona, Glenn said, "I'm not going." He had a job and money and he'd get his own apartment. And so he did.

I didn't want to go to Arizona either. I was going to be a senior. Don't make me leave my friends. So mom called my dad, which I know she hated to do. But she called him and he said yes. Yes, I could stay there. Yes, I could move in with him and Sheila, his beautiful young wife. Yes, there was room in their big house at 17th Place and Birmingham Avenue with Sheila's son Willie, who was twelve by now.

Willie, whom my dad had adopted. Willie whose name was my dad's name now. Only years later did I piece together the significance of that. For now, I was a stranger in a strange land.

Sheila always wanted a girl, so she set right to work and made me a beautiful bedroom with pink and green polished cotton bedspreads. The curtains matched and I had a window seat in the dormer. A fairy tale room.

Willie's room was across the hall. Just the two of us upstairs—upstairs!—and he was silly with excitement at having me, a sister! He showed his affection by shorting my sheets and reading my diary. He wanted to sleep in the other twin bed in my room and kept a ninja sword under the mattress to dispatch any intruder who might try to spirit me away. I'd only ever had Glenn, a big brother, worldly and cool, so I was unprepared for Willie's onslaught of affection and his unabashed desire to claim me for his own.

The doors and windows in Daddy's house sat square and solid in their frames. The toilet seats didn't wobble. The TV worked and the yard had real grass and flowers at the borders. Mature trees—magnolias and elms, spruce and maples—dotted the yards and shaded the streets that formed the neighborhood around 17th Place & Birmingham Avenue. Daddy's house was just as nice as all the houses around it and, indeed, every house in the quarter was nicer, stronger, and better-maintained than any other house I'd ever known.

Sheila was a marvel of a housekeeper—nothing like my mom, for whom such things were a distraction, tended to when they could no longer be ignored. But with Sheila, meals were pre-planned, if uninspired. Dishes were cleared away, washed, dried, and returned to their assigned cabinets after every meal. She changed the bedsheets weekly; the continual cycle of washing, drying, folding, and storing them was repeated seamlessly in her well-practiced system. She vacuumed or mopped floors and even wiped down the shelves in the fridge as a part of her constant motion. She seemed always to have a damp cloth in her hand. I saw no particles of dust in corners or on windowsills, and should any crumb stray onto the carpet, her ceaseless surveying found it out and rounded it up, post-haste.

Sheila had a player piano, an upright refinished to a honeyed sheen, and two shelves in the hall closet devoted to rolls of music that could be loaded into it. It was a marvel. The paper stretched scroll-like between two rollers and over a bellows. Once I flipped the lever, the roller engaged, and the paper, blank except for the perfect perforations arrayed across and down the extended, continuous page, passed over the bellows, activating the corresponding keys for "Moon River," or "The Old Piano Roll Blues." It generated full-throated songs by way of wind and percussion, somehow. It amazed me as much as my own playing might have, if I'd ever learned to play.

I sat on the piano bench after school when the house on 17th Place and Birmingham Avenue was empty and played melody after melody, creating flush harmonies without ever touching the keyboard. The keys themselves sprang to life, and "God Bless America" filled the room and the house, grand enough for Ethel Merman. Some of the rolls had the lyrics printed along the edge, and I sang along. At the end, always abrupt with the final chords ringing, hanging in the air, the roll reversed itself and sprung backwards, rewinding, whizzing back to its starting point. When I pulled the last roll from its position, boxed it, and returned it to the closet, a stillness settled into the rooms of the house, as though even I was not there.

My first inkling that all was not perfect at Daddy's house came the day I went to the downstairs linen closet to get a fresh tea towel for Sheila. We were cleaning up after tuna-fish sandwiches on a Saturday. Daddy was at the skeet range and Willie was outside with the kids next door. When I pulled the towel—creased and folded to display embroidered pansies along its edge—from the shelf, something tumbled onto the floor. A small box of matches. Odd. I picked it up and thought to return it to the shelf when I saw the cigarette there, a Virginia Slim. Just one. I took it and the matches, along with the tea towel, to Sheila.

When I handed those three items to her, our eyes met. "Oh," she said, "you've found me out." And then, "Don't tell your dad." She tucked the cigarette and matches into her apron and we returned to the cleanup. She gave me a couple of sidelong glances and a mischievous smile. I guess we were in cahoots.

After that, I found her stashes all around the house—a cigarette and matches in the laundry room behind the Tide, in her sewing basket in the den, among the canned goods in the kitchen—even in the freezer in the garage. I knew why she did it. My dad would not tolerate smoking. So they played a game. Now and then, when he'd find her cigarette and matches, they'd argue about it and she would again pretend to quit. For his part, he pretended not to smell the smoke on her breath or in her hair. He pretended to believe her.

Sheila took a tole-painting class on Sunday evenings. Willie went with her to play basketball with the kids of other adult students at the community center. So Daddy and I had the house, and the only TV, to ourselves. I wanted to watch *Laugh-In* so I could keep up with the conversations at school, but it came at a price—it was sponsored by Virginia Slims. When the inevitable ad came on, he put his arm around my shoulders, pulled me into an awkward angle and said, "Carolyn, you don't smoke, do you?"

I tried to look at him, but he was so close! "No, Daddy, I don't smoke."

"Good. Don't ever start. It's a nasty habit." With this admonition, he might jostle me a bit.

"I won't." Then I'd sit up again and he'd rearrange himself as well.

Week after week this ritual played out.

Daddy set strict rules to govern my comings and goings. He monitored the mileage on my car and stood at the door at midnight to review my state when I came in from my dates with Russell. He told me he could hear Buttons, Sheila's cross-eyed Siamese cat, when he crossed the living-room carpet, and he could certainly hear me if I tried to sneak around. So, soon enough, just like Sheila, I began to lie to him.

Maybe he only pretended to believe me too, I don't know, but at the end of my second year at 17th Place and Birmingham Avenue, before I could tell him that Russell and I were going to get married, he blurted, "You're pregnant!?"

He didn't know that Mom had already told me never to have kids. He didn't know that Russell and I weren't having sex, though we were on the brink. He didn't know that I wanted to marry Russell and move to California more than anything because I wanted to get out of that lovely house and away from him. I didn't know another way to do it.

Chapter Fifteen

Kenny's Leg

When Mom moved to Arizona and I moved in with Daddy and Sheila, Glenn moved to a tiny, funky rental house on Yale Avenue. There he lived his perfect hippy life with his hippy friends.

Sometimes when I went there, he asked me for money. I gave him whatever I had from working Men's Underwear at JC Penney.

He worked all around town, for a while at the Dairy Queen. He said the guys peed in the soft serve just for meanness.

Once the police came and searched his little house for drugs. They didn't find any, even in the ceiling tiles. That was lucky.

He dated Ginnie Baker. Cute and sexy. He said Ginnie's mom liked him until the day she came to his little house looking for Ginnie. She walked up the driveway to find him lying on his back on the hardened clay of the front yard, making an imprint of his body in the leggy weeds. Mrs. Baker stood at his head looking down.

"What are you doing?"

High on LSD, he floated under her gaze. He swam—a backstroke—or maybe he was making a snow angel. Happy and relaxed in the sun, he squinted and smiled at Mrs. Baker's upside-down face, patted the cracked ground at his side and said, "Come on in! Join me!"

Glenn didn't have to worry about Vietnam because of his diabetes. But everyone else was worried about it. The Army called up our friends by draft number. We gritted our teeth each night, not knowing what the news might be in the morning. The Mentzer twins had to go. Lou Cook had to go. Mitchell Henley went.

At 6:00 p.m. daily the networks broadcast scenes of soldiers wearing helmets with chin straps swinging loose, crouching, signaling each other, pointing their rifles across fields of rice, or lifting their comrades onto helicopters with menacing propellers beating the grass down around them. We saw them in jungles and swamps packing A-K 47s, their hollow eyes looking across the world into our guilty and fearful hearts.

Then they killed Phil Lewis. Phil Lewis died over there. A pall settled on the merry band. Glenn and the rest of Phil's friends huddled in the little house on Yale Avenue, passed a joint, processed the fact of Phil's death.

"Shit," Glenn said flatly as he put an alligator clip on the joint before he handed it off to Dave.

"No shit, shit." Dave had number 362 in the lottery. Lucky birthday. He wasn't going any time soon. Probably never. He had a student deferment too, and said he was thinking about medical school. Dave! But now, in this knot of young men, he took a hit, narrowed his eyes, and hissed air in with the smoke.

"Fuck," he said, still holding the smoke in his lungs, his voice a rasp.

He handed the joint, now just a roach, off to Gordon. Gordon with flat feet and a heart murmur: 4F. Gordon sucked the last bit of residue from the roach and pinched the clip open, tapped it on the tray where incense left a perfect line of ash from the night before when Ginnie was there. Glenn finished twisting the ends of the next joint and handed it across to Gordon, who deftly flipped open his grandpa's Zippo and lit up. As the smoke curled into Gordon's right eye, he passed the Oaxacan on to Kenny.

"I ain't goin' back," Kenny announced before he drew the sweet smoke himself. He sat cross-legged on the linoleum floor and held the joint. No one objected. Kenny was in the Army already, home on leave after boot camp, his once long, glossy brown hair now just stubble above thick eyebrows on his shiny skull. "I ain't goin' back. I'll go to Canada if I have to." He took another hit.

They were silent a while longer.

"Phil was a good man."

"If you don't go back, they'll come and get you."

"You'll go to jail."

"Army jail."

"Leavenworth." A groan, as if they knew the particulars of Leavenworth. Dave and Gordon shifted position, allowing blood to flow to alternate limbs.

"I don't care. I ain't goin'. I ain't gettin' blown to shit." Kenny took a long hit and lay back on the floor, his legs still folded. At last, Dave reached across and took the joint from him. Glenn and Gordon drained their beers. They all knew Kenny wasn't going to Canada.

"We could hide you."

"Where you gonna hide me?" Kenny said to the ceiling.

"My grandma's house in Pawnee! They won't look for you there!"

"Right. He's gonna live with your grandma. Is she a conscientious objector?"

"Naw, you guys can't get involved. You'll be in jail too."

They thought about the truth of that statement.

Then, finally, "What if you were sick?"

"Or, hurt?"

"Yeah."

The slow orange sun of an idea rose in the fog. Glenn got up and brought the last beers from the round-shouldered fridge visible from his cramped living room. Dave skillfully rolled another joint, lit it, inhaled, held the smoke, and started its circulation counterclockwise this time, letting Kenny go first.

"I'm not sick or hurt."

"What if some guy was in a car wreck? He can't go back. He's in the hospital, right?"

They leaned forward.

"If you were in the passenger side and got T-boned..."

"Oh yeah. Sounds perfect." Kenny sat up.

"We're gonna wreck a car?"

"Right. Be careful about the *car!*"

Silence. Kenny passed the joint to Gordon.

"What if you were sick?"

"I'm not sick."

"No, but they don't know that."

"If you touch a thermometer to a light bulb, it will show a high fever."

"Fuck man! I don't think the Army's going to let me stay home because I've got a fever."

More silence. Gordon passed the joint to Glenn.

"We could injure you and say you were in a wreck."

"I've always wanted to hurt you anyway." They laughed a tepid laugh.

"What kind of injury would it have to be?"

"You guys are nuts."

"No. What kind of injury would it have to be, to keep them from taking him back?"

Maybe Dave's medical mind kicked in. "I'm taking a piss," he said and got up and headed through the bedroom door. The rest leaned back in silence. Glenn picked at a thread on the arm of the sofa, thinking of Phil Lewis and Kenny. Gordon noticed the music had stopped and began shuffling through the cassettes. Creedence? Led Zeppelin? Lynyrd Skynyrd.

Glenn went again to the kitchen. "Hey! Twinkies!"

He tossed the package to Kenny who turned it over in his hands. "Nah, man, I hate these things."

"I got nothin' over here," Glenn said, opening doors to cabinets he knew were empty. Dave came out of the bathroom. "You got any money?"

Dave plunged into his front pocket, came up with a wad of ones and tossed them on the counter. They all began digging. Soon enough more ones, a couple of fives and a mound of coins lay on the counter. They looked at each other and grinned in unison, "Taco Bell!"

Gordon collected the offerings, straightened each bill and faced all the dignitaries in the same direction. He scraped the change, more than three dollars' worth, off the counter with his right hand into his left, and from there into the front pocket of his Levi's.

As he passed the stereo he cranked the volume up on Lynyrd Skynyrd, "Gimme three steps, gimme three steps, Mister, / gimme three steps toward the door!"

Out they went in comical formation with Gordon and the money in the lead. They piled into his grandmother's Chrysler and crossed the freeway overpass with cars whooshing below. At the intersection, they sat through a green light with Dave smiling his wide, gummy smile, "Taco Bell!"

"I love Tack-o Bell!" Glenn said. "Everything's the same. Just order by shape!"

"I want two rounds and an oblong."

"Throw in some semi-circles!"

"Gotta have an enchirito—oblong with sauce!'

At the next green light, somebody honked. Gordon flinched, glanced at the rearview mirror, and turned onto Admiral Boulevard. They crept along in the right-hand lane next to the curb and eased into the parking lot of Taco Bell, stopping only when the Chrysler's front tires hit the concrete bumper of the spot closest to the entrance.

They squinted in sequence as they shambled into the fluorescent space, raised their palms as if to the sun, blocking the overhead light to view the menu they knew by heart. In line, they bunched and laughed. "Gimme three steps and an oblong, please!"

They shuffled and jostled, tried to keep their laughs soundless, until the man ahead of them, in oily refinery dungarees and a blue flannel shirt, turned toward them with an orange plastic tray wobbling a tall cup of Coke and three tacos. His Texaco work jacket and black lunch box complicated the load. His face and hair were grimy and the left leg of his dungarees was split up to the knee. The denim fell open to reveal a cast from his knee down to the open toes, also grimy. The cast had a little heel built in and he tried to pivot on it, gyrating with the tray.

"Whoa! Here, let me help you with that," Glenn said and took the man's tray. "Where do you want to sit?"

The man nodded. "Thanks," he said. "The corner's fine. I can't get used to this damn thing." He took an awkward step toward the orange plastic bench. Glenn held back for half a step and gestured broadly with his head and eyes toward the cast.

"How'd you break your leg?" he asked, a little too loud.

Dave, Gordon, and Kenny were limp but standing. They watched Glenn and the man work their way past the Formica table tops to the window seat, staring, mesmerized by the cast.

"Thanks a lot, man," the man said.

"My pleasure," Glenn said and slid the tray onto the table. He turned back toward his friends and locked eyes with Kenny, then the others.

"That's it," he said, and they nodded. "Okay then. Let's get something to eat."

They huddled at a corner table and ate in silence, far different from their usual raucous outings, filled with laughter, spills, apologies, and once even a voluntary clean-up of all the tables with the night shift cashier's damp rag.

"Can you take it?" Glenn asked Kenny.

"Yeah, I can take it."

Glenn studied him a moment, then said, "I've got a bat."

Kenny unwrapped a semi-circle and crunched half of it into his mouth. Dave, Gordon, and Glenn drank long from their watery Cokes.

They drove back to the little house pensively, their grim mission in mind. Two-by-two they marched up the concrete steps with no railing, through the door with no screen. The stereo was silent and the house seemed to hold its breath. Glenn went straight to the fridge and brought out a fifth of Jack Daniels full up past the middle of the label.

"Drink this," he said, handing it to Kenny.

"You keep it in the fridge?"

"Yeah, I don't know," Glenn said, as he turned to the bedroom. He went into his closet, crammed with jeans and shirts and shoes and a Frisbee and a croquet set with a broken mallet. He came out with a baseball bat.

He sat next to Kenny and they all focused on the bat.

"Give me that," Glenn said and took the bottle from Kenny. He took a long pull and handed it back. Kenny took a long pull too.

"That is gonna hurt like shit," Dave said. Kenny drank again.

Ever the planner, Gordon said, "You better take some practice swings. You don't want to have to hit him twice."

Gordon looked around and went to the narrow space between the fridge and the wall and pulled out Glenn's unused straw broom. It had a sturdy handle. He braced it at an angle between the couch and the baseboard. Glenn stood, steadying himself using the bat as a crutch. Dave stood up next to Gordon and they backed away. Kenny sat stupidly on the floor.

"Like you're chopping wood, man."

"Yeah, up over your shoulder."

Glenn drew the bat back and it hit the overhead light fixture, neatly lopping off its finial and causing the frosty white cover to drop directly behind him. It broke into four perfect pieces.

Kenny pulled another long drink of Jack; Glenn kicked away the broken fixture and repositioned himself and the broom.

Dave and Gordon shifted.

Kenny's head began to loll.

"Go ahead, man," he slurred, his bloodshot eyes nearly blind.

Glenn swung back and brought the bat down hard, throwing himself off balance. The bat skidded down the broom handle to the straw. Kenny raised his head. Gordon and Dave stood mute.

"Oh, I've got it." Glenn positioned a folding chair across from the couch and put the broom handle straight across from the couch to the chair seat, parallel to the floor. He stepped back and, with the form of Paul Bunyan, swung the bat. With a sharp crack he split the broom handle in two.

They stared at the shattered broomstick. The sound of its splintering permeated the air.

Finally, Glenn said, "Last chance, Kenny. Do you want to do this?"

"Le's do it," he slurred. "I ain't gettin' blown to shit." He struggled up to the couch. Throwing his left leg onto the folding chair, he said, "Hit me man."

Dave and Gordon steeled themselves, looking on sideways. Kenny's chin poked his chest, the empty bottle of Jack still in his hand.

Glenn stepped back and once again swung the bat like an axe, as if he had chopped wood all summer. It hit Kenny's shin with the crack of a grand slam. Dave and Gordon pulled their arms up to their faces. Kenny screamed a silent scream, rolled onto his side and off the couch, curled up as he went, his shattered leg followed in grotesque asymmetry.

Between real screams, he vomited, heaving again and again, his body convulsing in horrible rhythm.

Glenn stood over him a moment, then he vomited too. Jack Daniels, Taco Bell, and Coors fouled the air.

Gordon and Dave made for the door. Dave threw up on the concrete steps. Only Gordon kept down his oblongs and rounds.

***

Kenny had to go back anyway. The Army didn't care about his leg; they had work he could do until he was ambulatory. When the guys repeated the story of that evening, we had no sense of foreboding or premonition.

Why would we?

Chapter Sixteen

The Price of Acid

The 51st Street Bridge across the Arkansas River stretched long and wide, smooth and flat, the newest connection east to west in Tulsa. Glenn took it for fun. There wasn't much of West Tulsa on the other end yet, but there was lots of good riding. Roller Coaster Road had its lure.

Once he made land on the west end of the bridge, he could fly north past 41st Street, 31st, on up to 21st, with no stoplight to slow him down, and deliver whatever he was selling. The day of the accident, it was LSD. He had a tiny envelope with 20 hits of blotter acid in the right coin pocket of his jeans. The blood didn't spread that far up on the right. His left leg was broken in 18 places below the knee, so blood filled his left boot and saturated the denim up to his crotch on that side. High up on the right, the envelope stayed dry.

On that sunny day he made his way along Skelly Drive on his Kawasaki 500, slipping gleefully between and around the commuters at 5:00 p.m. If they were going 60 mph, he was going 65. At 5:05 p.m., traffic flowed onto the bridge, then, without warning, stopped.

Mid-span in the left lane, Glenn saw the brake lights just as the cars ahead of him moved to the right, opening a clear view to the stalled car in his lane. With nowhere else to go, he applied his own brakes, leaned back and gritted his teeth. At the last moment, he swerved to the right and smashed his left leg against the bumper of the stationary car. The Kawasaki lay down, skidded across the middle lane and wedged under the driver's side door of a blue Datsun with a pretty blonde girl at the wheel.

Separated from the bike, Glenn slid into the middle lane himself, engulfed in a cacophony of screeching tires and twisting metal. The cars of the commute came to a stop, clustered around him as he lay in agony with a crushed leg and his blood flowing freely onto the fresh smooth pavement.

Commuters leapt to his aid, one man pinning Glenn's left thigh to the pavement with his knee in an attempt to staunch the sickening red flow. Others stood by, helpless, alternately looking down at him and then turning away.

A siren's cry swelled in the distance. At last an ambulance came into view, but slowed to a stop at the end of the bridge. EMTs left the ambulance and trotted along the emergency lane toward the center of the bridge like Marines in formation.

Commuters stepped back and the EMTs huddled over Glenn, now barely conscious. After a moment, one stood straight above the others, looked back toward the end of the bridge and pressed the button on his shoulder-mounted radio. "Get another ambulance here quick. This kid is bleeding to death." Glenn only learned later that the first ambulance had run out of gas.

In the second ambulance, the EMTs cut his jeans off with their stubby scissors, just like in the movies, missing that little pocket and the envelope. They rolled his jeans up and put them in a bag with his wallet and T-shirt, along with one blood-soaked sock and one dirty dry sock, and his motorcycle boots, one of them soggy and red as well.

That evening, my phone rang in Long Beach, California. It was Mom, her voice pale and distant. "This is your mother," she said from her rental house in Williams, Arizona. "Glenn's been in an accident."

Not comprehending the message, I sat mute.

"He's in Hillcrest Hospital. His leg is smashed. They might have to amputate. I'm going back."

"Mom?"

"He was on his motorcycle. I'm going back."

"I'm going too. Wait for me. I'll be there tomorrow."

I sat for a moment with the phone in my lap and thought of the last time I'd seen Glenn, in July of 1969, just two months earlier. He and Mom and Russell and I were playing Monopoly at her house in Williams. Russell and I were newlyweds. We had the aura of fresh beginnings around us. We had just driven from Tulsa in our '64 Chevelle convertible, having broken down only once, in Amarillo. We stopped to see Mom on our way to Long Beach and the USS Wichita, where Russell was stationed. Glenn was staying with Mom for a while and visiting friends in the area.

We huddled at the kitchen table with leftover tacos in disarray around the game board. Glasses of Coke sweated puddles onto the table's hard green surface. Doritos and salsa trailed salt, crumbs, and tomato splotches around the perimeter of the game, where pastel money was tucked under the edge of the board and deeds to property lay fanned out like playing cards.

We knocked Momma out of the game early. She was up clearing dishes and putting leftover Mexican into the fridge. She made forays between us, wiping up and folding paper towel coasters for our Cokes.

Glenn and Russell worked their acquisition strategies from the first roll of the dice. Glenn had all the Railroads and several monopolies on two sides of the board. Russell had the Utilities and key monopolies as well. I survived the first ninety minutes with scattered property and a series of lucky rolls, sashaying through the minefields of their holdings. It couldn't last.

When the dice next came to me, I used my "Get out of jail free" card and rolled a seven. Tap, tap, tap and my top hat landed squarely on Park Place. Russell owned the coveted dark blue monopoly and had hotels on it and Broadway. I wouldn't waltz out of this one. He simply held out his flattened palm, smiled, and said, "Pay up, Honey."

I surveyed my meager holdings, then made like Little Nell, placing an imaginary bow in my hair. "I can't pay the rent!" I said with the sweetest lilt I could muster.

"You must pay the rent," Russell said. Mom booed and hissed from the sink. "Don't be a cad!" she said.

Russell only looked at me and flexed his hand for emphasis. Then he coiled an imaginary villain's moustache, rolling his thumbs across his fingers below his nose. "You must pay the rent."

"Oooh, you're a big bad man," I said as I started to gather my cash and deeds in surrender.

"Wait," Glenn said. "I'll pay the rent."

Action froze. Mom turned toward the table. The implication was clear: Whoever acquired my properties would win the game. I had several odd lots that could finish out remaining monopolies around the board for Glenn or Russell. Any leftover odd lots would keep the other from ever completing his monopolies. My property was the key to victory.

Glenn, now remembering details of the melodrama, placed his imaginary bowtie at his throat, pushed his chest out, and repeated with pride, "I'll pay the rent!"

I looked from one to the other. I had to choose who would win the game: My beloved brother, or my new husband.

I can't say how I reasoned it through. Nor do I recall the details of what followed—if I stayed at the table or retreated. But Glenn won the game that day. And just like then, Russell was forlorn now that I chose to leave him alone in Long Beach and go to Glenn in the hospital in Tulsa. Russell and I had only lived together a couple of months in the roach-infested one-bedroom apartment in downtown Long Beach, where I now sat, numb with the news of my brother's injury. Russell was crestfallen, but I would go.

He took me to the bus station and stood on the curb in heavy diesel fumes as I settled into a window seat above him. I thought he would cry when the driver put that beast in gear. With an acrid hiss we began a slow roll out of the station. I placed my palm on the glass, but the bus turned away from Russell and there was no point in trying to see him now. He wouldn't be able to see me. So I settled in for the all-night ride to Williams.

***

Even with a fresh start the morning after Momma picked me up at the bus station, we were exhausted when we turned out of her driveway and headed east to Tulsa, to Glenn. The prospect of his injury drained us. The horrible specter of it. The colossal weight of it.

We must have stopped to sleep on the ride from Williams to Tulsa, but I don't remember it. We must have talked, but I don't remember that either. We didn't sing. Or play the license plate game or remark on the deer, or the trains or the clouds in the sky.

We left Arizona and pushed on through New Mexico and the Texas Panhandle and western Oklahoma until we came to Tulsa, and we did not stop until we were walking down the hospital hallway to his room and his bed.

Momma went in ahead of me and leaned down to hug him as best she could. That's when he saw me over her shoulder. He lifted his hand to me and said, "You came."

Maybe he wasn't sure I'd heard him all the way in California. But I did. In my bones I heard him. I took his hand and Momma stepped to the side. "Hey Bubba," I said.

"Hey."

Tears sprang to my eyes, but he looked okay. He shook my hand to wave off my worries. I turned from his face to see that the bedding was twisted across his body to reveal his leg elevated by a sling. It rested in a half-cast, a plaster of Paris canoe with his leg fitted down the middle and wrapped in blood-spotted gauze, a Civil War bandage. Metal pins protruded on each side at the top and bottom. It wasn't until days later that I learned there were exactly two pins, each about eight inches long. They ran through his knee and ankle, constituting the means by which the half-cast was held in place.

In the days that followed, doctors and nurses came and went. Mostly they wanted Glenn to wiggle his toes. When he did, it was a good sign. They unwrapped and re-wrapped the cast. I took him for strolls in a wheelchair, but the pain was so great that a seam in the floor could made him grip the armrests of the chair and grimace. I felt it too, up the backs of my legs, a flare bone deep.

Mom and I slept in chairs and went back and forth from somewhere, but I don't know where. It doesn't matter. What does matter is that when Momma and Glenn and I left the hospital five weeks later, we carried the bag with his bloody, dirty boots, his T-shirt and cut-up jeans, his wallet and the blotter acid. But not his leg. It had been broken in 18 places below the knee. They tried, and they might have saved it if not for the diabetes. The bone and tissue would not heal. Bad circulation and all.

Chapter Seventeen

Phoenix Airport

After the amputation, Glenn and Mom and I retreated to northern Arizona—Williams, and her rented house. We huddled together, and cooked and ate and played Monopoly; we watched TV, drank beer and cheap wine. Glenn's friends took him out to get high. Mom's friends came by the house and we made nice.

She couldn't convince him to leave Tulsa and move back in with her permanently, or even for the time being. And anyway, he had to return to Tulsa to be fitted for Peg, as he'd already named his prosthetic leg-to-be. So Mom and I drove him down to Phoenix to catch a plane home.

We sat on either side of him in the boarding area with a crowd of folks waiting and watching the plane on the tarmac, when a little girl seated on the floor across the aisle fixed her gaze on the space where Glenn's left foot used to be. She looked up to his face, then to mine and to Mom's. Eyes wide and features slack, she did not return our smiles.

Raising her sticky palm to her wispy hair, she looked again at the space below the hollow leg of his jeans. She didn't turn her face away from us, but she reached toward her mother, pulling hair with her hand as it went.

Her parents looked across the rows of vinyl seats and restless passengers to the concrete of the runway and the white Arizona sky.

"Mommy," she said, and patted her mom's shoe top, "Where's that man's foot?"

Her mom and dad followed her pudgy pointing finger, turned toward our faces, then Glenn's leg and back to our faces. They drew embarrassed breaths and bent toward their daughter. Passengers around them turned to look as well.

"Oh honey!" her mother said. She picked up the girl and stood in one motion. Her husband stood too, gathered his newspapers, the child's baby doll, and her sweater. As they hustled away the mother turned and mouthed "Sorry!"

***

No covered walkway that day. Airline crewmen in blue pants and blue shirts leaned into a rolling stairway and shoved it up to the plane's door. They locked its wheels, loped up the stairs, stood on the platform and pounded on the hatch until someone inside opened up. The three seemed glad to see each other; they laughed for a moment before the crewmen descended the stairs and stood at the bottom, as though to greet boarding dignitaries. Just then, the attendant at the podium took up her microphone and announced the start of boarding for Glenn's flight.

Mom and I kept strong as we helped him get situated with his crutches and his saddlebag carry-on slung across his body. Mom patted his chest and held his arm tight. He told us time and again he was okay. At last, he steadied himself, planted the crutches' rubber feet ahead, and began the measured process of swinging his body forward, placing his right foot, rebalancing, and again placing the crutches in front for the next swing.

People made room around him. Mom and I moved to the plate-glass windows, stood and watched in agony with tears in our throats. He wasn't the first in line, and after they cleared the exit door, one by one, other passengers broke and circled around him to get on board faster. A few hung back and matched his pace. A small conga line formed behind him, not gleeful but circumspect, slow but not impatient.

When he reached the bottom of the stairs he stood aside and gestured for the last few passengers to go ahead. The crewmen seemed to ask if he needed help, and he must have said "no." He placed the crutches against the bottom step and bent his knee. Suspended on those aluminum posts, he pushed against the crossbars and raised his foot. He almost hopped onto the first stair then pulled the crutches up as fast as he could. Once steady, he braced them against the next step and looked up. Nineteen more to go.

Two members of the flight crew, young women in navy-blue skirts and sky-blue blouses, stared from the doorway above. Glenn bumped and hopped onto the second stair and the third.

Below, the crewmen stood mute. They waited and watched as he worked his way up the fifth step and the sixth. Why didn't they go up and stand behind him?

Midway up the slant, after he pulled his crutches up to the step, he swayed back for an instant and I cried out. Mom grabbed my arm, and I knew it wasn't only to comfort me. We clutched each other; our eyes never turned from Glenn's climb.

He steadied himself again and a breeze lifted his fine hair off his shoulders. We could see his shoulders rise as he took a breath before he pressed forward with renewed determination. He didn't waver or wobble again. When he reached the platform at the top, the stewardesses parted and, never looking back, he disappeared between them as though through a portal to another dimension, another world.

***

From Sky Harbor Airport, Mom and I caught I-17 and settled in for the drive north, back to Williams. Through the glare of the desert flatlands we were quiet, tapped out. What was there to say? Glenn was on his way too, in the air above us. Maybe he had a window seat and was looking our way. I imagined two pins on a map, diverging.

Then, as we began the climb up toward Camp Verde and then Cottonwood, the scenery greened and the air began to thin. Pressure eased within us, too, a bit, and we began to talk about the red rocks of Sedona. Mom said she had a painting planned and hoped she could get the light just right.

By the time we turned west out of Flagstaff I started to think of Russell. How long had I been gone? Three weeks? Five? I hadn't called him in several days. No doubt he'd be drunk. Still, I knew I'd catch the Greyhound sooner than Mom would want and return to Long Beach, completing the distribution of our three-person family across the Southwest.

Chapter Eighteen

Glenn's Coney Island

The day of the accident, Glenn's care had been critically delayed when the first ambulance ran out of gas. With the money from that settlement, Glenn bought a house and married Donna. He bought a new Kawasaki and, even with his prosthetic leg, continued to ride. The pin in Peg's hinge at his left knee scratched a pattern into the gas tank when he shifted gears.

If he still thought about the day of the wreck, he never mentioned it. He didn't avoid the bridge or hang back in traffic. He loved riding as much as ever. But I never crossed the bridge again without marking the spot when I passed it.

With the rest of the money from the settlement, Glenn set about creating a business that would support himself and Donna and two other employees, our cousin Hale and Donna's sister, Louise.

To fix up the new place, Glenn and Hale did all the work they could, and they were pretty handy with carpentry and drywall. Terry Stephenson laid the carpet in the office. Mitchell, home from his tour of duty in Vietnam, pulled the wiring, and Jim Cunningham plumbed sinks and toilets. The friends worked through the night, night after night, and at their regular jobs each day. During breaks they sat on the dusty linoleum floor, smoked pot, snorted cocaine, and went to work again, rocking along with Waylon Jennings or Lynyrd Skynyrd.

Open for business at last, Glenn and Hale worked shoulder to shoulder. Or, more accurately, shoulder to chest. At six-foot-three, Hale stood seven inches taller and outweighed Glenn by 100 pounds. Strangers might not have understood their attachment, based on their physical appearances, but would rue the day they underestimated the power of that bond. These cousins stood together, thought things through together, acted in concert, created and sustained Glenn's Coney Island. They made it go, and go it did.

In the first week of operation, Glenn and Hale ran the whole show. They both opened. They steamed the hot dogs. They bought gallon tins of chili and bags of grated cheese. They reconstituted onions and heated the buns. Soft drink syrup canisters and the ice machine required their steady attention. Whoever was closer at the time did the duty. They took turns boiling spaghetti for chili three-way. Each signed for cases of Fritos for chili pies and ripped and collapsed boxes for the dumpster.

By that Sunday, their first day closed, they knew the business would go. It would make money. The Coney's location tapped into the construction boom in South Tulsa. Tradesmen came in their boots and jeans, basketball T-shirts under open plaid flannel shirts with the sleeves rolled up to the elbow or cut off at the shoulder. Their square hands and tan forearms bespoke strength borne of steady, repetitive motion—pushing beams, swinging mallets, pulling conduit.

They arrived in crews of five or more, loaded their plastic trays with the Coney's fare, filled and refilled blue wax-coated cups with carbonated drinks and crushed ice. They sat like loggers at the picnic benches and curled their backs over the tables, laughing and flashing white teeth as they ate. Burly and strong, they ate for a reason, and Glenn's Coney Island met the need.

During lunches that first week, Hale and Glenn perfected a choreography of side-steps and hand-offs, an intuitive call and response, a rhythm of coordination delivering sustenance to the troops of roofers and pavers expanding South Tulsa.

Sunday, their first day off in six, they met at the Coney to take inventory. Stationed at the picnic table closest to the cash register, Glenn sat with thick stacks of soiled bills arrayed by denomination in front of him. A mound of coins weighed down the end of the table near the wall. As Hale approached, Glenn unzipped a third red vinyl bank bag. Wads of cash swelled forward like so much haggis.

"You look like shit," Hale said.

"Thanks."

"My feet hurt!"

"Mine too. I'll get us some of those big rubber mats to stand on back there."

Hale watched for a moment then unzipped the fourth bag and began to sort bills from his side of the table.

They dumped the coins onto the end of the table, straightened their backs and stared at the booty. Slow smiles lifted their features. They shook their heads in wonder. Oh, this place would make money all right.

"We shouldn't keep this much cash here."

"Right," Glenn agreed. "We've almost paid the rent already." They shook their heads again.

Glenn counted out $500 in twenties and set it aside. "That goes toward rent," he said. He counted again and pushed $500 toward Hale. He took another $500 for himself, folded the bills in half and pushed them down into his front pocket. Piles of loot remained between them.

They not only would have to replenish paper products and foodstuffs, they would need more help.

From that day forward, that table served as their conference room. They counted currency and change, reviewed the day or the week, prepared bank deposits, talked about customers, drank Cokes, ate Coney's, and laughed and laughed.

***

Not long after came the day of the tornado. On that day, patrons of the strip mall scurried to their 'fraidy holes ahead of the menacing clouds that churned and surged from west to east across the Oklahoma plain.

"Gimme Shelter," began to fade out on KAKC. "Oh, children! It's just a shout away! It's just a shout away!" The DJ switched from cracking wise to the National Weather Service. "Listeners east of the Arkansas River near 81st Street should take cover now. Funnel clouds are confirmed in the air, but none yet on the ground as this volatile band of storm clouds pushes east, crossing through Tulsa at 18 miles per hour."

Glenn's Coney Island sat in South Tulsa east of the river, on 81st Street, the bull's eye of the storm's target.

Glenn and Hale stood at the counter and watched gusts of wind heave across the parking lot. A lady's skirt pitched up, exposed her pantyhose and inverted her slip. Stinging debris swirled around her ankles. She clutched her vinyl handbag, bent low, and tried to get her key into the door of her car.

A teenager made her way across the lot. She gripped the top of her head with her left hand as though she were trapping a wig. Her hair stood up around her hand in the frenzied bursts of wind. In her right hand she gripped a leash connected to her black and white puppy, a spaniel. He leaned away from her. Confused, frightened, he crept at her side.

The sky blackened and rain crashed onto the scene. It flew hard and fast, parallel to the ground, assaulting the strip mall. The plate glass window that formed the storefront of Glenn's Coney Island began to bow in toward the transfixed young men. It bulged, concave, as the vacuum created by the colliding fronts pushed outside in, toward implosion. A rumbling, now a roar, overtook all other sound. Glenn and Hale dropped below the countertop without ceremony.

Before they could speak, silence rushed in and sat heavy and ominous around them. They raised their heads and peered across the room, now black and still, eerie. Anticipation held them motionless. Then Glenn spoke.

"Let's get outta here."

"Don't wait for me," Hale agreed.

Glenn fished in his jeans pocket for the keys to his van as he hustled haltingly across the dining area and to the door with his prosthetic leg. Hale flipped a series of electric switches and loped toward the door behind him. As they crossed the threshold, Glenn slammed the door and threw the deadbolt. They made for their cars. Hale headed toward West Tulsa; Glenn went east-northeast.

He buzzed north to 71st Street in his hollow, white '72 Ford Econoline van before turning east ahead of the storm. When he crossed Lewis Avenue, he looked to his left in time to see a funnel drop from the clouds and skip along the ground, keeping pace with him. The long, thin funnel bent into an s-curve; its tip hopped back and forth. Like an enormous, mechanized sewing needle, it zigzagged across the neighborhood, choosing this house, then that one, to demolish in a brutal blitz. Lumber and rooftops and trees burst into the air in a surreal symphony of destruction. Boom! Boom! Boom! Power poles splintered in dreadful rhythm. Electric transformers exploded, flashed in brilliant accompaniment.

Glenn pulled his head down and shoulders up, gritted his teeth and clenched the steering wheel; as he jammed the gas pedal to the floor, the van whined, and again he found himself ahead of the front.

Oral Roberts University, to Glenn's right, lay quiet at that rise just between the inhale and exhale. Its huge geometric panes of iridescent glass reflected the murky grays and muddy greens of the squall. At that moment, in the rearview mirror, Glenn saw the cyclone traverse the thoroughfare, smash those mirrors into thousands of shards, and twist their frames into grotesque new sculptures before it rose into the firmament.

Glenn zipped along to Sheridan and turned north toward his little house on Florence Avenue. As he relaxed his grip on the steering wheel, blood flowed again through his shoulders and hands. He watched his rearview mirror until he felt certain the twister would not pursue him home.

The storm seemed to have made a decision. It lifted its sucking foot and released its hold on Tulsa. The clouds slipped eastward, rumbled, tossed threats back over their shoulders with flashes of lightning on the undersides. The afternoon sun lit the clouds' trailing edges with magic glowing gold. As if they pulled a giant tarp west to east overhead, the storm clouds left clear blue sky in their wake. People emerged from their basements and turned their faces upward, smiled at God, filled their lungs with electrostatically cleansed air. Safe for the moment at least, Glenn's mind turned to the storm that lay ahead: Donna.

He turned the van onto Florence Avenue and eased up the tree-lined block of 1940s cottages and bungalows. The van's tires swished along the freshly washed pavement.

Twigs and leaves littered the street and neighbors' yards. He could see Donna's car in the driveway of their house. The house itself looked dark, and he wondered if the turbulent storm had knocked out their power.

Just then Donna stepped onto the porch and, seeing him, waved him off the driveway. So he parked on the street, and, by the time he opened the door to the van, she was backing out. She angled past him, waved again, almost absent-mindedly, as she headed down the street.

"Great," he thought as she turned at the end of the block. "Great."

He started the van and pulled it onto the two crumbling concrete strips of their driveway, over the pothole at the crest of the hump, and onto the flat next to the porch. The adrenaline of his flight from the tornado, the anticipation of an encounter with his wife, and the reversal of that expectation left him depleted. She was gone more and more, it seemed. And even when she was home, she was absent.

He sat in the van for a moment with no thought, no energy, no plan. Rivulets of rainwater trickled down the windshield in front of him. Pico, the Weeny Wagger—next door's bulky black-and-white Tuxedo cat—hopped across the driveway as though he could keep his paws dry.

At last, Glenn eased himself out of the driver's seat, negotiated the steps up to the porch, crossed its faded, flaking paint, and unlocked the front door. It opened directly into the living room. He hesitated, looking from the living room straight through to the converted dining room, all the way back to the kitchen.

The musty air stood still but retained a sense of his morning encounter with Donna. Glenn stepped into the living room and paused again, clicked the door shut before he moved toward the interior of the house. To his left, papers protruded from beneath the couch cushions. He pulled one out. The water bill. He lifted the cushion to reveal a wad of junk mail, correspondence, other bills, and their checkbook register. He took it in hand for a moment and looked at Donna's handwriting slanting across each narrow page.

"Manor Mortgage," she'd written in large looping letters. This created the sole entry on the top half of the register. No amount was recorded, nor was there a balance carried forward. On the lower half she'd written, "Penney's, $23.51," across four lines and "Hoolihan's" in the margin below.

Glenn shook his head and dropped the register back on the pile. Checks were there too, torn from the book, corners bent, some with dates on them but no payee. Others with payees but no dollar amount or signature.

He let the cushion fall back into place and moved toward the dining room, his wooly recliner, and the TV. Waylon uncurled from his tucked position in the corner of the couch. They looked at each other for a moment; then the cat warbled his sweetest greeting. Glenn had to smile.

"Hey, buddy." He sat on the edge of the recliner. Waylon hopped onto his lap. Glenn scooted back into the chair and pushed back, extended the leg rest. They settled into their routine; the cat pushed his pink nose into Glenn's hands and dragged his lips across his palms. Glenn scratched every surface Waylon presented, massaged his paws, rubbed his belly.

From there, Glenn could hear the radio playing in the bedroom he shared with Donna at the back of the house. Pat Benatar. "Hit me with your best shot! Why don't you hit me with your best shot?"

He let his head fall back onto the cushion and his muscles released their last bit of tension. In a moment, he was asleep. Waylon stretched out toward Glenn's feet, closed his eyes, extended and retracted his claws, worked the denim of Glenn's jeans before he softened into his own escape.

Chapter Nineteen

Lost Sight

Russell and I had one year together before he shipped out to Vietnam. We explored Southern California, and I wrote home about beaches and falafels and traffic and Hollywood and *Hair*. I shopped at the Navy commissary and ironed his dress whites.

I took him to the USS Wichita every morning, and, once, I went out with him and other sailors' wives and their children for a "family cruise," courtesy of the United States Navy. That morning we milled about on the deck of the gray metal behemoth with much anticipation of our day at sea. Sailors hoisted the gangway aboard and wound giant ropes into the hull. They called to each other and scurried about and disappeared below decks. We listened to the Captain's welcome and made small talk with families standing close by until I became impatient. When would we ever get started?

Then, at that very moment, I turned, expecting to see our car in the parking lot, the trucks and cranes and mighty containers stacked at the water's edge, but the shoreline had receded! Unmonitored, undetected, the land had drifted away. I stood dumbfounded. No sensation of movement revealed the ship's seaward headway or the land's retreat. But the continent had slipped toward the horizon, widening the gap of ocean between. Now I stared, processing my disjunction, disbelieving. Before my eyes and without a sound, the rift expanded.

I think that is what happened in our marriage.

When Russell shipped out with the crew of the Wichita only weeks later, it didn't occur to me to move back to Oklahoma. I would wait for him in Long Beach.

Maybe young people should not marry only to be separated for a year at a time; for, while he was gone, I learned things a young wife should not know.

I learned I could live on my own, away from parents, from high-school friends, from my husband. I could go to work and make money and pay rent and feed myself and buy short skirts and big sunglasses. I could go out with new friends and get high. I could listen to loud music and sing just as loud. I could take a joint from the guy on my left and smile at him when I took a hit and pass it on to the guy on my right and smile at him too. Sometimes, I was the prettiest one in the room. I had the longest hair and the longest legs.

When Russell came home from his first tour of duty, he'd had his own life, too, for those thirteen months. He'd been smoking and drinking and going on shore leave with his shipmates, all wound up and seeking release. Hong Kong and Manilla offered an education for him just as revolutionary as mine in Long Beach. He and I were doomed by those days. Though we weren't yet conscious of it, ship and shore had begun to part.

When I was alone in Long Beach, Mom called daily from Williams to talk about her day and mine, and to relay Glenn's news—he had a new car or a different motorcycle. Or business at the Coney was good, but it looked like he and Donna might split.

Then one day she called to say his vision was clouding. He went to Oklahoma City for a specialist who told him that his diabetes caused capillaries in his eyes to burst and bleed into the vitreous humor. The blood muddied his view.

They cauterized those capillaries, and, within a few days, his vision cleared. But it happened again. More veins erupted and more blood oozed in. Another round of cauterization and a few months of clarity.

Round three was different. The doctor said that soon enough, the cauterizing would have the same effect as the bleeding. Each burn site left a scar, and scars could not receive light. The treatment for clouded vision was blinding him.

Filled with anxiety and yearning pain, once again I left Russell and took the bus from Long Beach to Williams. Then Mom and I drove the familiar roads back to Oklahoma City to be with Glenn and bring him home on the turnpike to Tulsa, the three of us stunned and searching the future. What now? How could we be realistic and optimistic and practical? Our conversation came and went in awkward fits interspersed with wretched stillness.

We distracted ourselves with stories of the mundane: a student of mom's who kept bringing her apples and flowers; southern California's smog. Glenn told us he met a Candy Striper at the hospital.

He said he sat up on the edge of the hospital bed to take his meals. After his surgery, a young volunteer came in with his breakfast and sat on the bed beside him. She pulled the rolling tray across his lap. He still had his peripheral vision at that point, so, if he turned his head slightly, he could just see her in the corner of his eye—dark hair, rose lips, starched white shirt, and pink-and-white striped apron tied snug at her waist.

"My name's Marie," she said. "I'll help you with your breakfast."

She put her finger through the center hole of the metal dome and lifted it from the entrée. "We have scrambled eggs, toast, a carton of milk, apple juice, and an orange for later."

"Yum!" Glenn said with mock anticipation.

Marie opened the cellophane package containing sterilized cutlery and a stiff, one-ply paper napkin. Glenn sat at attention and waited while Marie positioned some scrambled eggs on the fork.

"Here come some eggs."

Glenn opened his mouth and, feeling the fork go in, closed his mouth around it. Marie then pulled it out clean.

And she took a bite for herself!

"I think the eggs could use a little salt and pepper," Glenn said.

Marie just swallowed; her shoulders came up as though to shirk off her guilt. "Yes!" she said, and she snapped open two tiny, corrugated paper packets and sprinkled the seasonings over the eggs. Then she arranged another bite for Glenn.

"Here it comes." He opened and closed again. While he chewed, Marie took a second bite as well.

"How about some toast?" she offered.

Glenn nodded his head. "Any butter?"

"Yes, there's butter, and let's see, it looks like grape jelly. Want some of that?"

"Sounds good," Glenn said.

Marie peeled the foil top off the tablespoon-sized container. She spread the softened butter over the cold triangle of toasted white bread and repeated the procedure with the tablespoon of jelly.

"Okay, here you go."

Glenn took a bite and reached up, indicating he could manage the toast on his own. While he took another bite of toast, Marie had a third bite of eggs.

"Milk?" he asked.

"Sure." She pinched open the carton, stripped the wrapper off the straw, and put the rig in Glenn's hand. He was glad to have control of the toast and milk, not to be fed like a baby.

"More eggs?"

"No," he said, and resisted the urge to say, "You go ahead." But no matter. She did. They finished the last few bites of his breakfast in silence.

I asked him when he told us this story if he called her on eating his breakfast or reported it to the nurse in charge.

"No," he said. "She must have been pretty hungry."

With that we passed through the turnpike gates into Tulsa and made our way to his house on Florence Avenue. We coached him out of the car and up the steps to the porch. And now he sat in his wooly chair with gauze taped over his eyes, felt for the phone and the clunky box that functioned as the TV remote control. Donna was nowhere to be found. Glenn said she had all but moved out.

Mom and I made lunch and Glenn tested how it was to eat food he could not see from a plate he could not see. More than once he brought a fork to his mouth only to discover that the bite of casserole had fallen off during the journey.

"What's on that list the doctor gave me?"

It was post-op follow-up instructions. I began to read the list aloud and most of it was common sense: Keep your eyes covered. Don't allow soap or shampoo into your eyes. But an item a third of the way down said, "Avoid turning your head unnecessarily." Why hadn't they told us that? Glenn had been turning his head as anyone would in conversation! Why, he'd reacted with a jerk to an inadvertently slammed door. He'd leaned over the arm of his chair to retrieve a dropped fork! This could be bad! I shot a look at Mom, who was stricken.

With stiff arms, Glenn pushed himself back into the chair and forced the footrest to swing up, but he didn't relax. He sat with his head rigid and neck unbendable.

Mom and I fussed over him and busied ourselves cleaning and rearranging, distracting ourselves from the facts: soon his remaining vision would be gone. Maybe he should have kept his head still, but it didn't really matter. He would be blind regardless.

Russell called, and I said I didn't know when I'd be home. Glenn needed me. I'd stay until we got him settled into a system that worked for him. Our cousin Hale and Glenn's buddies—Dave, Greg, and Mitchell—had already begun to coordinate their visits, coming by morning, lunchtime, and evening. Teetum shopped and cooked and put groceries away. Glenn would have to learn how to find things and put them back. Yes, I'd come back to Long Beach, but not yet.

Mom had been quiet, preoccupied. She bustled about one morning, then left for the drug store and came home a long time after we'd begun to wonder and worry—in a taxi. She'd wrecked her car, she said. Totaled it. She never saw the guy coming on a wide-open stretch of 11th Street and pulled right out in front of him. He was going almost 50 and slammed into the driver's side of her car.

Bruises formed large blotches of purple and black below her left shoulder and elbow. Her neck was stiff and her left hip and ankle, too. Aching, she said, but not broken. She had a knot on her head where it had snapped into the driver's side window. They checked her out at the hospital and let her go. It took way longer than she thought it would.

"You should have called!" I cried in wonderment.

"No," she said vaguely. "There was nothing you could do."

With that she went on to bed and slept well into the next day. She crippled around for a few days like Walter Brennan of *The Real McCoys*. She was fine, she said. She'd be fine.

We never thought how much like a stroke her accident was: blindsided by a slam out of the blue, left side debilitated.

***

Russell called again, but I wasn't ready. Mom would have to get her insurance and get another car. Then I'd drive back to Williams with her and ride the bus back to Long Beach. I'd let him know. Questions must have arisen. How could I stay gone for so long? Did I miss him? At my end, they weren't so much questions as realizations: It was easy to be gone. My life with Glenn consumed me. I thought of Russell only when he called. The ship had drifted; the shore receded.

Chapter Twenty

Spiral Staircase

After Daddy left and before the TV broke, Mom and I watched Liberace together and *Perry Mason* and Leonard Bernstein. "From the ridiculous to the sublime," she would say.

I felt proud and secure to run the gamut with her, talking to Della Street on the screen, or lifting my chin with Leonard. I loved to flip my imaginary coattails when I sat at our second-hand upright piano. I tried to flaunt my wrists like Liberace. But I couldn't play.

We watched movies on TV, too. *Laura, Rebecca,* and *The Spiral Staircase.*

There's a scene in *The Spiral Staircase* in which the murderer, a serial killer who targets women with afflictions, sees Dorothy McGuire, who plays Helen, a mute. The lower half of Helen's face is blurred to depict her debility.

The killer watches her from behind the spiral staircase and is enraged by the blur. Something's wrong. She cannot speak! The killer sees only her incapacity. She will be his next victim! We know why he chose her to kill.

At that moment, the killer's eyes burned. And just then, when we saw through his eyes, Mom turned to me, tucked under her arm, and said, "I think that would be the most terrible thing, not to be able to speak. I hope that never happens to me."

I didn't understand the flicker of fear in her eyes or the flat look that followed, but knew she went inside herself in that moment. It passed quickly. We turned back to the movie and all was well.

Momma had moved to Northern Arizona, to get away from her exes, she said. I had married Russell to get away from my dad. To get an education, and to put off settling things with Russell, I moved to Santa Barbara, went to UCSB. Momma called me every day from Williams, and we talked for an hour or more. Every day.

"This is your mother," she would say when I picked up, and off we'd go. She wanted to know all the details of my schoolwork. She prompted me for every minute of my part-time workday at Santa Barbara Janitor Supply, and then she'd say, "Why don't you quit that stupid job and come live with me?"

Then a day came when she didn't call. She didn't call Glenn in Tulsa or me in California. It was a Friday. She always called after school, but not that day.

Glenn called me that evening to ask if I'd heard from her. He was already worried. He had called her and gotten no answer. It was unusual, but we agreed she'd probably gone out to dinner with her friend Bobbie or Wesley. We would hear from her later.

But we didn't hear.

Saturday morning, Glenn called again. She still wasn't picking up. He got Wesley's number and called. No answer. No answer at Bobbie's. We waited—Glenn in Tulsa and me in Santa Barbara.

Finally, Wesley answered and agreed to go check.

She never locked the house. He said he went in calling, "Lucy? Lucy?" He went straight to the bedroom and found her there, unconscious. A wastebasket at her bedside contained junk mail and vomit. The bed was wet with her urine.

An ambulance took her to Williams Hospital. Six beds and a GP. They understood right away that she needed more than they could provide, so they loaded her back into the ambulance and sent her to Phoenix, three and a half hours away.

Glenn called and said, "She's pretty bad."

"What am I supposed to do?" I cried. He didn't know.

I dropped the phone in Santa Barbara and went to my bed. I think I must have been wailing when suddenly she floated before me. Stunned into silence, I watched her face on a black screen. Her eyes pleading. The lower half of her face blurred like Dorothy McGuire's in *The Spiral Staircase*.

"Is this what you want for me?"

"No!" I cried out. "No."

And she was gone.

In that moment the phone rang. It was Glenn, his voice small and distant. "Mom didn't make it."

She'd had a massive stroke. "Cerebral infarction." Had she lived, she would have been immobile. Unable to speak.

Later a call came from Teetum. "Carolyn, your mother's on her way back to Tulsa. She's going to Moore's funeral home. You need to come on home, too."

Momma made the trip alone. I didn't know how. In a box? A casket already? Whose cargo was she? Was it a bumpy ride?

Teetum had done everything on her own as though Glenn and I were small children. She set the date and time for Momma's services. She chose the flowers and the music. And she picked the dress Momma would wear for eternity. I don't often think of my mom's body in her grave, but when I do, I think of that ridiculous dress.

Glenn and I said to bury her in her University of New Mexico sweatshirt. That's what she loved. She wore it nearly every day. She was proud of it and comfortable in it.

But Teetum would have nothing of the kind. You don't bury people in sweatshirts! She would go shopping and take care of it. She called later to say she'd found a pretty dress for mom. It was green with lace. Lace sleeves. I could not imagine it.

I read *The American Way of Death* in my high-school senior English class. So when Teetum called to say, "You need to pick out a casket for your mother," I was ready.

I told Glenn all about the scandalous methods those people used to squeeze the most money out of their customers, preying on the aggrieved when they were most vulnerable. They would lead us past the cheap caskets kept in darkened corners to the best lit, most beautiful, most comfortable, most water-tight, most expensive casket.

Glenn and I agreed that we would not be led like ignorant lambs. We had a small inheritance and Mom wouldn't want us to spend it on a casket.

With that, Glenn and I went coffin shopping. I wore my white flair-legged pants and a sky-blue cotton shirt. He wore his jeans with the rabbit pelts sewn into the seams to make bell-bottoms.

Mr. Moore greeted us at the door.

He could see our pain. His voice was cool and even. He walked us through a showroom with faint music wafting just within our hearing. He spoke in soothing tones about what would be most appropriate for our mother.

He steered us past remote corners of the showroom. What reflected her sensibilities? What would we like to remember for the remainder of our days? We were charged with choosing her last resting place.

We bought the best lit, most beautiful, polished ash, the most comfortable satin-lined, most water-tight, and most expensive casket.

I said ignorant things about Mom's dead body: I don't need to see it. I don't want to see it. What a bizarre ritual it is to go and look at a corpse. Everyone knows that is not the person. It's an inanimate object. "We are a superstitious lot," I said, arrogant even in my shock and pain.

But when the moment came, the last moment at the funeral, the moment just before they were going to close the lid and take her away, I had to go and see her. I wanted to see her one more time.

So I went to the side of the beautiful ash-wood, hand-lacquered, satin-lined casket and looked in.

She looked terrible. Her hair seemed thin. It wasn't thin in life, but there was her scalp reflecting the tasteful dim light of the funeral parlor. Her chin pulled in as though she might be trying to look down at the top button of her shirt, and that angle gave her jowls. Her lips turned down in a grim expression.

And the dress. The green prom dress Teetum had bought for her. Lace sleeves. My mom wouldn't be caught dead… Sherbet green. Lime sherbet. Kiwi. It was satiny too, or shiny grosgrain. The lace of the sleeves extended from her shoulders down her arms to points that ran onto the backs of her hands, lying crossed on her belly. The bodice was snug around her middle and I had the feeling the dress couldn't be zipped. She was going to her grave with the zipper open down the back of her party dress.

"Momma!" a sob escaped me. I reached out to clasp her hands. Thick and icy cold, they stunned me.

"So cold!" I said, and at once I was transported into myself. The words echoed inside my head, "So cold." For an instant I stood in a hall of mirrors facing each other. A thousand images—of me, the casket, my hand on hers, her lips, her downcast eyes, her chin—extended to infinity. So cold, so cold, so cold.

Chapter Twenty-One

Coma

I woke and let my eyes travel the walls of the room and began to assemble the present. Where was I exactly? Where had I seen these walls, covered in aluminum foil and umber-stained for effect? I lifted my head. That wall's a floor-to-ceiling mirror. Orange shag carpet? Oh.

I remembered.

Just days before, I visited each of my instructors at UCSB and told the story of my mother's death and my brother's blindness. I cried again and again and got their blessings to go, to abandon my education, California, my marriage. I loaded the U-Haul and pulled away from student housing. I felt glad, relieved, that Russell wasn't there to watch me go, that I didn't have to see him, forlorn again—still—to reconfirm my detachment and his self-loathing.

Curled in my lap, Lulu, my tortoise-shell kitty, a stray I coaxed from the filth and fear of her own crushing world into mine. Folded up and stacked behind me in the U-Haul, nine years of set decoration and play-acting. In the rearview mirror now, that time receded as I turned east out of the parking lot.

That's right. I was in Tulsa. At Glenn's hippy house. My marriage had failed. My mother was dead. My brother was dying. Down the hall. He was dying down the hall.

Okay! Up and at 'em!

Six days in and I was pretty good at those insulin shots. No biggy. I didn't feel a thing.

Glenn barely had to wake up before I tossed back the covers and swabbed a spot on his white thigh, all efficiency and competence. We had just about hit our rhythm. "Here's your shot."

But this morning, the sixth morning, was different. Within moments of my sticking him with that tiny needle, he lost consciousness. He retreated before my eyes like smoke sucked into a vacuum. I shook him and called his name. I rushed to the edge of panic, grabbed his shoulders and shouted, "Glenn!" His head lolled away from me. I grabbed the lemon drops from his bedside, unwrapped one with trembling hands and forced it into his mouth. No response. He was sinking. I could see it.

I raced down the hall and called the only adult left to me—Teetum, on the west side of Tulsa. "Glenn's unconscious."

"Okay," she said. "We're coming," and hung up. I sat on the bedside, stroked Glenn's forehead and cried. I was there less than a week and already I had killed him.

Impossibly quickly, A.L. and Teetum burst into the room.

"Why didn't you call an ambulance?" A.L. said as he wrapped Glenn in a blanket, picked him up, and carried him out the door like a bride across the threshold. I don't know why. I didn't even think of an ambulance. What's wrong with me? He was dying and I'd killed him.

Glenn's breathing was shallow as we sped toward Hillcrest Medical Center. Teetum drove her Caddy fast, like an ambulance driver. She honked, took whichever lane she needed. Glenn lay across the back seat, his body shifted this way and that as the car swayed from lane to lane. I sat in the front between Teetum and A.L. with her big vinyl purse in my lap and his leg touching mine. I struggled to end the contact even then, even in that moment.

We roared up to the Emergency Room entrance at Hillcrest Medical Center where I was born, leapt out of the Caddy and opened the back doors. Green-clad emergency room personnel swooped toward us with a gurney and Glenn was on his way. A young ER intern focused on me and said, "What happened?"

"Insulin," was my feeble response. "No breakfast."

He understood, turned away from me and loped after the gurney and my brother.

They saved him that day. Turns out, "Insulin/no breakfast" is a snap for them. And I didn't make the same mistake again. Glenn and I rocked along for a good stretch of time without another skirmish with disaster. I had vaulted out of kindergarten for caregivers, all the way to junior college. A brusque initiation. I would join the varsity squad soon enough, and then—semi-pro.

Chapter Twenty-Two

White Kitty, Dead Kitty & Mom

Patti Lee had tickets to Bob Dylan. We talked about it for weeks. Glenn said he was glad I was going to go. Happy for me. How cool it would be. How much fun.

But as the day of the concert drew closer, his anxiety rose. Sure, Hale would spend the night with him. Dave would come by. It was fine. It was okay. "Go," he said. "I'll be fine. Of course. Go!"

Then, three days out, he said his chest felt tight. No biggie. Just that he needed to catch his breath, that's all. We smoked a joint that night but he laid off after a couple of hits. "I'll stick with beer," he said.

Two days out, I re-confirmed that Hale would take care of Waylon as well as Glenn. He knew where Waylon's food was and the litter box.

Glenn pulled his shoulders up when he breathed. Is he doing that on purpose?

He is.

He's trying to keep me from going. He's working the guilt.

I don't care! I'm going. Everything's in place and I need a break and it's Bob fucking Dylan and I'm going!

The day before the concert, Glenn couldn't breathe well at all. Shallow puffing. Then he coughed a wrenching, gagging cough. I sat on the arm of his wooly recliner with my palm on his back until, at last, the spasm passed. He went to bed.

I called Dave and described the coughing. "That's not good," he said, and I knew he was right.

I wanted to go to Oklahoma City with a bare midriff and see Bob Dylan and dance in the aisles and stay the night and drink and smoke dope and have fun.

But I wasn't going to get to go. Glenn was getting sicker and sicker. I would need to stay with him.

Now my chest felt tight.

Glenn slept fitfully the night before the concert and so did I. A swirling saga of a dream engulfed me: A dark, moonless night. A field. People, ominous forms, all black and faceless turning toward me. Their voices swelled but I could not understand. Humming. Dread. Then, a fire. The field filled with fires glowing. All around me. Suddenly, a sinister voice, close, in my ear: "That cat is dead."

I woke with a start to Glenn's gagging cough and listened as the nightmare receded. This did not sound right. I trotted down the hall and flipped on the overhead light to see him writhe to his side and gasp for air. And the cough did not relent. He could not draw a breath deep enough to ease the wracking convulsions.

"Glenn?" I went to his side and again put my hand on his back.

He raised his head slightly in my direction and coughed and coughed. He lifted his hand toward his mouth, tried to speak, but could not manage it; the spasms would not allow it.

I ran down the hall and called 911. Here we go.

By 4:00 a.m. he was sedated and sleeping almost upright in Room 623 at Hillcrest Medical Center. His breaths came in short, shallow bursts, his mouth popping open and closed with each one.

Across from the drip bags and the heart monitor I pulled my feet up and leaned to the side in the hospital's version of a cushioned chair, resting my head on its wide wooden arm. In a moment, I slept too.

When I woke, a nurse was at his bedside with the tube from a drip bag in her hand. She released the clamp and fluid flowed into my brother. The nurse glanced at me. Smiling a sympathetic smile, she left the room without a sound.

Seven o'clock. My eyes burned. I stretched my legs, both knees cracked. Glenn turned in my direction.

"How's it going, Bubba?"

"You're here," he said. His face was colorless; his lips dark. I took his hand and brushed his hair back, giving him a big forehead. He smiled and huffed short breath after short breath.

"Hungry?"

He shook his head "no."

Tears rushed to my eyes and I was glad he could not see. We squeezed each other's hands; I was careful not to squeeze too hard. He had no energy to speak, and neither did I. Neither of us knew what to do.

We didn't move, but stood in relief, monochromatic in the dim hospital light. A still life. A portrait of trauma.

When his hand relaxed I let mine slip out, but stroked his shoulder and arm before moving away. Just then, a doctor came into the room, flipping the light on as he crossed the threshold.

"Hello," he said, glancing at me then taking Glenn's chart from the end of the bed. He stood silently, head bent. He lifted a page, stared a moment and let it drop.

"Hello?" Glenn croaked, almost a whisper.

"I'm Dr. Duma, Glenn. It looks like you had a rough night."

"Dr. Doom?" Glenn rasped this time, managing a smile.

Dr. Duma glanced at me to confirm the joke. "Not the most comforting name for a doctor, is it?"

Glenn gasped and coughed a shallow cough. Then he coughed again and again. Dr. Duma went to him and leaned him forward, adjusting the electronic bed so that Glenn sat upright, T-square.

"I know it's hard, but the coughing is good. It can help you expectorate the fluid and phlegm in your lungs."

Glenn nodded as this bout of coughing subsided. "Fluid in my lungs?" he rasped.

"Yes, pneumonia. You have only about 20% of your lung capacity. Your heart's enlarged as well."

"What do we do now?" I asked.

Dr. Duma looked at me obliquely. "I'm Glenn's sister."

He nodded and said, "Antibiotics. Rest."

We were silent then. The doctor fidgeted with his pen and made a note on the chart. He looked up and said, "I'll be back around this afternoon." He nodded again, replaced the chart and left.

Glenn pushed his head back into the upright pillow and mattress. He pulled in short breaths, his shoulders pinched upward. I put my hand on his chest and he covered it with his hand.

"Try to rest."

He nodded, each intake of air a small skirmish. "I'm going to go home and feed Waylon."

He reached for the pillow and tried to wrench it to the side of his face. He managed a resting spot for his cheek, bent his neck to the side and slept.

***

Waylon chirped his funny little chirp when I opened the door. He wound around my ankles and we wobbled and wove our way into the kitchen. I gave him his Kitty Queen Kidney, his kibble and fresh water and left him engrossed in the moment.

I wanted a shower but instead sat in Glenn's wooly recliner and pulled the phone onto my lap. I had to call Patti Lee and beg off the concert. I needed to call Hale and Dave and all the guys so they would go to the hospital and sit there with Glenn. But before I picked up the receiver, I cried and cried. I sobbed. I wiped my nose on a Taco Bell napkin and cried some more.

It felt good, the release. It felt okay. Finally I pushed back on the arms of the chair and reclined. The weight of my body surrendered to gravity and defeat and knowledge of the next battle.

Just then Waylon hopped into the chair with me. He licked his chops and purred with his mouth open. I moved the phone and he took his place on my lap with a quick turn. He rested his head on his paws and in an instant we both slept.

***

When the phone jangled two hours later, it was Glenn. "Where are you?" he said.

"I fell asleep. Are you okay?"

"Yeah. Dave's here; Hale will come by when he gets off work." He'd already been up, calling, rousing the troops. They were responding.

"Let me have a shower and I'll be right there."

"No, you'd better get your stuff together and get to Oklahoma City. Patti Lee and Bob are waiting for you."

"No. I'll stay with you."

"Don't be stupid. I'm fine." He coughed for a long minute and came back on the line. "See? I'm okay."

"I can't go when you're in the hospital!"

"It's the perfect time to go. Nothing can go wrong here! I've got all the help I need."

I paused. He was right, but... "You're sure?"

"GO!" He coughed and coughed for a long time, the handset on his lap. I listened with a clenched heart. Then he composed himself and said it again, "Go."

"I love you Glenn."

"I love you too. Have fun."

"I'll stop by on my way to the turnpike."

We hung up and I looked around the room, taking it in as I contemplated my escape. Ashtrays with cigarette butts and roaches; "little toot" with residue of cocaine; cable box with cord strung across the shag carpet.

Porsche in the driveway.

Suddenly, I understood that I was glad he had to be hospitalized.

There it is. I was glad.

Not just relieved, which would have been bad enough. How can a caring person, a sister, ever feel relieved that her brother has to be hospitalized?

But in fact, I was beyond relief. I was happy. Free.

He was ensconced on the 6th floor of Hillcrest Medical Center with nurses padding about and a call button at the ready and I felt good.

He was well cared for and safe. I could go. I could get drunk and party. I could go see Bob Dylan.

I wanted to drive fast and far with the music loud. I wanted to fly away. I didn't want Glenn to call me on the CB radio as I blasted down the road in my black Porsche.
No Glenn. No diabetes. No blindness.

Waylon now sat framed in the door to the hall and stared. My nightmare flooded back to me.

"Uh-oh buddy. We have to make sure you're okay while I'm gone. We don't want any dead kitties."

Waylon followed me around as I checked his kibble and water dish again. I cleaned his potty box.

"No in-and-out privileges," I said and closed the window he used to come and go at will.

Then I cleaned up, threw my things in the car and rolled backward down the driveway. By the time I got to Room 623, Dave, Mitchell, Arnold and Greg were there, looking scared; smiling; acting tough.

Glenn looked spent. Paler than ever and small, so small. My throat swelled and tears filled my mouth. I stood at his side and kissed his forehead, turned, looked desperately at his strong healthy friends.

Go, they said. We've got this. He'll be fine tonight. Go. You should go.

So I turned and ran. Down the hall, into the elevator, through the lobby, into the Porsche. When I got to the turnpike entrance Linda Ronstadt came on the radio. "You and I travel to the beat of a different drum / Oh, can't you tell by the way I run / Every time you make eyes at me?"

I cranked it up and flew.

***

Our seats for the concert were crappy—literally behind the stage. We were close though; right at the edge of the stage, looking at Bob's back and into the lights like he was. The backs of the amps, all in silhouette; his curly hair made a glowing halo like the cover of *Blonde on Blonde*. Now and then the bass player or drummer would turn in our direction. Bob showed his profile.

We had a good buzz going, tequila shots at the house and Oaxacan on the ride to the Lloyd Noble Arena. We passed joints up and down our row of seats and sang, "'Come in,' she said, 'I'll give ya shelter from the storm.'"

The night swirled. We swayed with the cramped crowd behind the stage. We played air guitars and sang as loud as we could sing, "I want you! I want you! I want you. So bad!"

Someone fell. It didn't matter. We jostled. We strained to hear Dylan's voice until we knew the song, then we sang again. "They'll stone you when you're tryin' to be so good. / They'll stone you just like they said they would."

On and on it went. Arms in the air. Lights glaring. Mumbling at the mike. And bursts of song again. "It ain't me babe! No! No! No!"

And suddenly, the lights went out. Uneasy silence. Some shuffling onstage. A strum. A swell of sound from in front on the stage. What were they saying? We swayed on our feet. Was the equipment buzzing?

Then a flame in the darkness. An orange light. And another. Then a dozen more. And a hundred. Breathless silence. Lighters. Pockets of flame. Fires glowing all around me.

The dream. Oh no. The nightmare. What's happening?! No, no!

Then only his voice:

"How many roads must a man walk down…" A roar from the faceless crowd. A solitary spotlight. "…before you call him a man?"

Screaming. Buzzing. Fires. Fires all around. Closing. Close.

"Let's get out of here," I said to Patti Lee. She didn't hear me, couldn't hear me. My tears flowed. I grabbed her hand. "Let's GO!"

Together we ran, Bob Dylan's voice growing faint behind us.

"How many seas must a white dove sail / Before she sleeps in the sand?"

***

The guys left and the hospital grew quiet after visiting hours.

Glenn said he could hear the nurses' voices rising and falling from their station adjacent to his room. They alternately spoke with authority, murmured or chuckled, then fell silent.

He kept the volume of the TV low and remained upright, following the doctors' orders. He drew shallow breaths. His swollen heart labored.

The air conditioner repeated its rhythmic lull and the monitors behind his head hummed and beeped their own hypnotic pulse. He drifted.

Then, to his left, he heard her voice, questioning, calling. "Grenn?"

What? What was that?

"Grenn?"

It was Mom's affectionate mispronunciation of his name. He raised his head and turned to listen more closely. Suddenly he felt warm, relaxed.

Then he said, she was in him. "In him" was the only way he could explain it. He felt her presence within his chest. She lifted his hand, and with the pad of his ring finger touched the spot between his eyes where her mole was, the one she touched absently in life, that very same way.

She loved him. He felt her love.

And she went to work. He felt her moving inside somehow. Warmth. Light? Pressure. Release.

He observed it, felt it. His heart. His lungs. What was happening? He stroked his own hair, caressed his own cheek. Then his hands came to his chest and settled. He drew a deep breath, calmed, his head again on the pillow; and with an apology, she was gone.

***

Our footsteps clattered on the hard granite of the arena hallway. Security at one doorway took a step in our direction, then turned to watch us run. We drove, drunken and stoned, on freeways and surface streets, through dark neighborhoods and bright clusters of commerce. We turned in and out of cul-de-sacs, hugged the curb, sped and drifted until we arrived at the home of a guy Patti Lee was excited about, Derek. By the time we arrived, his party was jumping.

We stood on the porch, rang the bell again and again and waited, leaning on each other, until at last, the door swung open and the partiers in proximity turned to stare. Derek emerged.

"You made it!" He held his arms out and back like airplane wings, leaned in to kiss Patti Lee, his tongue leading.

"This is Carolyn," she said when they broke apart.

He swooped toward me and I dodged left. His lips grazed my hair and he pulled back, surprised that anyone wouldn't open arms and mouth to greet him.

"Hi Derek," I said.

Unabashed, he stepped between us and put an arm around each of our waists, pulling us into the melee.

A guy in Levi's, cowboy boots, a vest but no shirt turned from the wet bar with margaritas in his hands. To his dismay, Derek took the drinks for us and we moved on, past French doors and a swimming pool; wet people screamed with laughter and pulled each other into the pool as they fell, beer bottles and joints in hand.

We turned into a grand room full of party goers and the Rolling Stones blaring, "…never be your beast of burden…" Guys turned to look at us and Derek said, "Yeah, boys! That's right!"

We smiled too and drank it all in.

Derek steered us into a paneled library. He turned to kiss Patti Lee again.

I stepped away and began to peruse the shelves. He had a mishmash of books. Rows of hardbacks and paperbacks. Some textbooks. He must be an accountant. Unopened classics, a set, leather bound and gilded, pristine. A boxed set of Time-Warner books, each about a different artist. These looked well-used; van Gogh out of his box and leaning on Dali. Pages torn from Warhol lay askew on the shelf.

At a break in the shelves I found a large framed portrait not of people, but of two cats taken in that very room, the walnut paneling forming the backdrop. A black cat reclined and a white cat sat upright next to him. Both gazed at me serenely.

Just then Derek was at my side. "Are these your cats?"

"Yeah," he said, weaving in place, looking appreciatively at the portrait. "Little Kitty and White Kitty." He pointed

to the black one and said, "Little Kitty's around here somewhere."

"What about White Kitty?" I said.

Derek leaned in close to me; his chest pressed my shoulder, his lips on my ear. His breath was sickening, a stale mix
of daily bourbon and cigarette ash. I recoiled, but he pulled
me closer.

"That cat?" he said, his mouth at my ear. "That cat is dead."

I think I was blind for a moment. No, I was in the dark
field, the nightmare. The buzzing and the fires all around.
The voices, unintelligible. The dread.

"Oh," I said, and my knees buckled.

Derek caught me in my armpits. Even then I was
conscious of his hands too close to my breasts, but
my protests were unintelligible. He steered me to a
couch where he let me go. I pirouetted and fell into
the posture of an ingénue, ankles crossed and hands
in lap. But the room swirled and I wanted to run
away.

The rest was an embarrassing mixture of people fawning over me, fanning me, asking me questions. They
brought water and Doritos and bean dip and in time I
sobered up.

***

I woke mid-morning back at Patti Lee's house, the return
trip a blank. I collected my things while she slept sideways
across her bed.

I showered, made coffee and drank it; ate toast with grape
jelly and wiped up the crumbs.

Standing over her again I said, "I'm heading out."

She stirred, opened her eyes and waved.

***

Dr. Duma shook his head in wonder as I came into Room 623.

Glenn was sitting up. The TV was on and he drank water from a cup with a straw. A breakfast tray showed evidence he'd eaten.

A nurse coiled the tubes from the drip and looped them over the T-bar. She smiled at me and shook her head as she rolled the contraption toward the door.

"Oh my gosh," I said. "You look good."

"Mom was here," he said.

"What?" I looked at the doctor.

"I've never seen anything like it," Dr. Duma said. He clicked his ballpoint and slid it into his pocket.

"Mom was here last night," Glenn smiled at me. I took his hand. "I think she healed me."

"What?"

"We're sending him home," Dr. Duma said. "His lungs are clear. He's good to go."

She didn't heal him, of course. He said that's why she apologized as she left. She wanted to do more.

But he was breathing normally. The doc said his heart sounded pretty good.

We got home at mid-afternoon and Glenn called the guys. They brought quarter-pounders and tacos. OU played Texas that afternoon and Waylon slept in Glenn's lap all day.

Chapter Twenty-Three

Rejecting the Budgies

Glenn watched a lot of TV. There wasn't much else for him to do after he rejected the budgies.

At some point after all the doctors agreed that he would not regain his sight, the hospital sent Social Services out to meet him, to put on an encouraging face, to offer suggestions and books on tape.

It's hard to say what that woman might have been thinking when she arrived at our hippy den that day. The cottages on Florence Avenue, with their redbud trees and thorny hedges, like most houses on most streets, gave few clues to the lives of their inhabitants. Maybe, from the porch, we seemed middle-of-the-road.

Right on time at one o'clock she stood under the white glare of the Oklahoma sun. I watched her for a moment through the gap in the frosting of the windows in the front door. She tugged at her jacket, but kept it buttoned. Navy blue, matching skirt. Probably lined. In this heat! In the

Oklahoma humidity! The weight of the briefcase slung over her shoulder dug a groove and bunched the fabric around the strap. Panty hose and pumps—she might as well have been wearing a hat, veil, and white gloves. She tried the doorbell, realized it made no sound, and then knocked.

She looked so prim and determined. That's probably why I took some pleasure opening the door in my bare midriff, baby-blue halter top and short-short-short cut-off jeans.

I invited her into the darkness of the living room and walked barefoot ahead of her through the archway into the converted dining room, where Glenn sat in his woo-ly recliner across from the TV, the cable cord looping through the shag carpet. One pane of the double window behind him housed a two-ton air conditioner rumbling at full throttle, giving the room the atmosphere of an airplane in flight.

The remaining three panes of the window, stuffed with newspapers, sealed with aluminum foil, and draped with a tablecloth of Indian paisley nailed around the perimeter, completed the ambience.

"Here's the lady from the hospital," I said.

Glenn smiled his benevolent smile and positioned his hand midair. She leaned down just a bit and reached out to shake his hand, but at that moment the briefcase strap slipped off her shoulder, yanked her arm down with it and the case itself clunked onto the floor.

"Oh! Excuse me. Gosh!" she struggled to collect herself. Meanwhile, Glenn's hand drifted downward until, back in order, she straightened up. Not to leave him hanging she reached for his hand and pulled it up with hers, shaking all the while. Once again, he turned his face upwards and smiled.

"Gloria Sherman, Hillcrest Social Services," she said.

"Nice to meet you. This is my sister, Carolyn."

We smiled perfunctory smiles and I gestured for her to be seated on the couch. She chose Waylon's favorite napping spot. Oh well. Navy blue and everything.

She lugged the briefcase onto her lap and rested her forearms on it. I decided not to ask, but assumed she'd want a cold drink and excused myself through the swinging barroom doors into the kitchen.

"I understand you had your own business," I heard her say as I pulled glasses from the freezer and Cokes from the fridge.

As I filled the frosty glasses and paused for the foam to settle, I heard Gloria Sherman tell Glenn, "Social Services has several self-employment opportunities they can help you with." I set the Cokes on the tray I used to take Glenn his meals, pushed the swinging doors with my back, and pivoted into the dining room. I did a partial curtsey near Gloria Sherman to offer her a Coke.

"Oh! Thanks!" She set her clipboard aside and took the tall glass. Her fingers melted ovals into the frost. She took a short swallow and looked for a place to set the glass. We never did get that coffee table we talked about. After a second sip she leaned forward and screwed the base of the glass into the shag until it felt stable next to her feet. Then she relaxed and sat back.

I went to Glenn's side table, rested the tray on its edge, and began to clear a spot for his Coke. I hadn't noticed that his "little toot" was on the table, more than half-full of cocaine. I put it in my pocket. Crushed Marlboro butts crowded his heavy amber glass ashtray, and a roach in a clip leaned into one of the corner grooves. I set the ashtray next to my Coke. I moved his sisal coaster to the side of the table closest to him and put his Coke on it.

"Here's your Coke," I said.

He raised his hand and I directed it with my free hand until he touched the cold glass. He took it in his grip, held it in place, memorized its position. "Thanks."

"My pleasure," I realized I hadn't turned the TV off as I'd planned to do. So I crossed the room to bump the power button with the flat of my hand when I saw, on the shelf below the Sylvania, our orange and blue plexiglass bong. This I swept onto the tray and made my exit.

"Oh that cold Coke hits the spot," I heard Gloria Sherman say as I set the tray on the kitchen counter. She continued in a pleasant, matter-of-fact tone as I put the roach and clip on the windowsill, dumped the ashtray, and patted the pocket secreting "little toot." Glenn turned his face toward me when he heard me come back into the room with only my own Coke in hand. "Ms. Sherman thinks I can continue running a small business," he said.

"Really? What kind of business would that be?"

"Budgies," Glenn said.

"Parakeets, actually," said Gloria Sherman, a little flustered. She leaned toward me with brochures in her hand. "We have several opportunities for unsighted individuals. You won't get rich, but you can make money supplying pet shops in the metropolitan area."

I took the brochures from her and began to flip through them. I glanced at Glenn, and I saw that he had that look, that little half smile that took over his features when he found something deeply funny but had to maintain decorum. I smiled a little half smile as well.

"How would it work?" I asked.

"Social Services helps with the set-up after his credit check and the initial investment. He would need a sighted person to assist, of course." Gloria Sherman couldn't keep herself from assessing my potential for assistance. She looked from my face to my flat belly and my tan legs. My toenails were painted "Hot Mama Pink."

I didn't care how Gloria Sherman assessed me, for she had tripped the switch of my disrespect when she referred to Glenn as "he" when "he" sat in the same small room, blind, but not deaf. "Unsighted," but not stupid. For this reason, I no longer looked at her or talked to her. I spoke only to Glenn and excluded her from my field of vision.

We went on a few more moments about the birds, their cages, their care and feeding, the finances of the operation, with Gloria Sherman looking back and forth between Glenn and me. Neither of us ever made eye contact—he because he couldn't; I because I wouldn't. No matter how many times she referred to the parakeets, Glenn came back calling them budgies.

Confused and exasperated, she looked toward me again and said, "What do you think?"

I looked at Glenn and waited. He didn't know it was his turn to speak, so I prompted him, "What do you think,

Glenn?" Gloria Sherman held her eyes on me another moment then turned toward Glenn.

"Aren't you afraid they'll turn on you?"

"What?" she said.

"The budgies. Don't they get sick of being in cages? What if they rose up and turned on you?"

Gloria Sherman, dumbstruck, stared into his unseeing eyes. She then turned to me, and this time I stared back, awaiting her response.

Seeing I would be no help to her, she sputtered, "Well, if I'd known you had an aversion to birds! Let's see," she plunged into her briefcase with both arms. "We have other options you may find to your liking."

Leaning down, squinting into the briefcase, her hair fell forward and she shifted her feet, spilling her Coke over her feet and into her navy-blue pumps. "Oh!" she exclaimed. "Oh no! I apologize. I'm so sorry."

"Not to worry," I said, scooping the ice cubes back into the glass and fetching damp tea towels from the kitchen. I gave her one for her feet and dropped the second one on the spill, blotting it with the ball of my bare foot.

"Can we call you?" Glenn said.

Gloria Sherman stopped her fussing and stared at him.

"We'll look over the papers and call you," he said.

She paused another second, realized she was being dismissed, and said, "Oh. Sure. Of course. My contact information's on the back of the brochures. Here's one more opportunity you can think about."

She handed me a brochure entitled, "Raising Worms for Pleasure and Profit." I pinched my tongue between my molars and stood aside as she rocked back to gain enough momentum to rise from the sagging cushions of the couch.

Glenn said, "Thanks for your time," as I walked her back through the living room and opened the front door. When she stepped into the sunlight I saw the big round patch—like a target—of Waylon's white cat hair, clinging to her left buttock.

***

Glenn wasn't afraid of budgies and he wasn't interested in worms. He didn't care to listen to books on tape, though we received the cumbersome recorder and bulky cassettes designed to assist the visually impaired.

He showed no motivation to learn Braille. His neuropathy had rendered his fingertips all but numb. We made a failed effort at tagging his collection of music cassettes using a label gun that created raised letters on stiff sticky tape. Here's Stevie Ray Vaughn. Here's Elvin Bishop. But he could not make out the letters or words. In the end, he made requests and I filled them. It was a good system.

He settled into a routine of smoking pot and watching TV. The University of Tulsa accepted all my transfer credits from UCSB, and I picked up classes to complete my bachelor's degree.

Maybe if he were going to live longer, we would have tried harder to overcome. But our mom was dead. Our marriages had failed. He was blind and very sick. We knew the trajectory.

Better for now to pacify our brains.

Chapter Twenty-Four

Las Vegas

I.

On the morning of our flight to Las Vegas, I threw up in the backyard.

We had planned and re-planned. Made lists, checked off items, shuffled and reshuffled. It was not the same as when able-bodied people planned a trip. On an airplane. With a blind man. On medication. In a wheelchair.

I could think of nothing else to do that would make us more ready. And now I needed a clear moment, free of questions, to breathe, to steel myself for our trip.

So I stepped away from Glenn and out of the house, onto the uneven surface of our patio. It was shady there and littered with sticky pink clusters from the canopy of our mimosa tree. But instead of refreshing me, the momentary coolness brought release in the form of spit up. I lurched forward, splattering clear liquid and white curds onto the concrete and the toes of my espadrilles.

I held my position, leaning from the waist, stiff-legged, holding my hair, staring at the river rock embedded in the concrete, and waited.

But that was it. All done.

I wiped my mouth, stepped back into the kitchen, wet a paper towel and swept it across my lips. Then I swiped my shoes and ankles and shins. I rinsed another paper towel and pressed it to the back of my neck. After it warmed, I crushed it and chucked it into the trash, vaguely aware that it would be dry and yellowed by the time we returned.

Drawing a breath, I tossed my head, threw my hair back behind my shoulders, pulled my chin up, and turned toward the front of the house.

Glenn hadn't been to Las Vegas since he lost his sight, but he talked about it all the time. "It's open right now," he'd say between downs of the OU–Nebraska game. "It's always open," he might say as I connected bottles of dialysate to the tube in his abdomen. "No matter when you think of it, someone's spinning the roulette wheel. Someone's shooting craps."

So I bought him a mini version of a craps table and a battery-powered roulette wheel. Dave and Hale and Mitchell and Greg would come by and smoke and play for nickels or toothpicks or sometimes even folding money. Glenn never tired of it.

We'd talked about going for a while, but his dialysis got in the way. We ran the machine three nights a week. The longest spell between its refreshing, full-body, peritoneal rinses was from Saturday morning disconnect to Monday night reconnect. So that's where we started our plan.

We calculated between tokes: If we ran the machine Thursday night instead of Friday night, that would buy us a day. We could fly out Friday, gamble Friday night, all day Saturday, all day Sunday—come home Sunday night.

Wait. We could come home Monday! That's right. Our regular dialysis schedule was Monday, Wednesday, and Friday night.

So we could stay till Monday! That's four days and three nights! That's a trip to Vegas! It's on! Let's do it! Let's go!

Glenn picked up the phone immediately and called Dave. "We're going to Vegas!" A pause. "Yeah! Don't know yet. When can you go?"

I could hear Dave's voice. He sounded good. Excited.

"Okay!" Glenn said. "Call me back."

He kept the receiver to his ear, pushed the button in the cradle, released it and dialed again. "Hale, we're going to Vegas! Can you go?" He paused, then, "Don't know yet. When can you go?"

Hale was softer spoken, but I could hear his murmurs. "Okay!" Glenn said again. "Call me back!"

He turned his face to me. Unseeing, he still seemed to see me. He grinned, his face lit from within. "We're going to Las Vegas!"

Then he asked, "Do you think Mitchell will go?"

Mitchell. Mitchell. My love. My undoing. Mitchell. Could Mitchell go? His work schedule as an electrician was flexible. It was his brother's business, after all. Would he go? His wife would be the deciding factor. Let's be honest. She was the overseer of our affair.

Mitchell and I had been an item since Halloween.

As soon as the sky darkened on All Hallows Eve, gypsies, ghouls, harem girls, Richard Nixon, Sonny and Cher, and other run-of-the-mill hippies streamed into the house. It jumped with bass lines and guitar riffs. Its windows glowed under the black canopy of redbud and Catawba. John Fogarty saw a bad moon rising. The devil went down to Georgia.

We smoked and drank tequila and Coors light and Bud and Oly. We did the Monster Mash. We howled with the Werewolves of London. Now and then, during a lull in the din, we'd hear a knock at the door and give handfuls of Tootsie Rolls to trick-or-treaters who'd been determined enough to make themselves known.

Glenn wore a blue bandana tied across his forehead and my white peasant's blouse tucked into his pants. We put patches over both his eyes and thought it was funny. I bought him a plastic parrot and pinned it to his shoulder. He kept a glow-in-the dark sword at his side and brandished it when he called out to new arrivals, "Ahoy!" or "Avast ye blaggars!"

Dave stuck close to Glenn, keeping him in the conversation and sharing his joints. Hale and Greg spelled Dave through the evening. I checked in with Glenn. I was Nurse Goodbody, after all.

At last, the revelers began to drift away. Only Arnold and Kathy remained in the kitchen. In our funky den it was down to Dave and Hale and Glenn in his fuzzy recliner and me. We turned the TV on, but left the sound muted. Lynyrd Skynyrd filled the air with their yawning, haunting lead guitar riff and baleful warning: "Ooh that smell! /

Can't ya smell that smell? / Ooh that smell! / The smell of death surrounds you!"

Just then, the front door opened and a mummified party-goer stepped in. We all turned toward the sound. No part of the mummy's body was exposed. He was completely bound with white crepe-paper gauze. Only beefy work boots escaped the binding. His hands and head were covered. Over his face he wore a skeleton's mask.

He paused, then came closer, into the living room.

Glenn tilted his head and listened. The mummy stood motionless.

"Who's that?" Glenn said.

"I don't know," I said and got up. The mummy stayed silent, still. I went toward him and said, "Who is that?"

No answer.

We faced each other, the mummy and me.

Feeling dubious but loving the joke, I said, "Well this is creepy!" I stepped up to the mummy and put my face near the skeleton's hollow eyes. The mummy had wrapped even his face and encircled his eyes with black, black eye shadow. His eyes were brown, gleaming, intense.

A thrill surged through me. Involuntarily, I flinched and grabbed his upper arms. He flexed and I felt the pulse of his biceps.

"Boo!" he said. With feeling. Ridiculously, I jumped back, but he now held my arms. He pulled me to him and I had to look into those eyes again. But now they were filled with mirth. Twinkling.

"It's Mitchell," Glenn said, recognizing his voice from that one syllable.

With that, Mitchell lifted the skeleton's mask and stretched the crepe paper away from his face.

"You scared me!" I said.

"I know!" he laughed, studying my face in a way that I would come to yearn for.

He joined the remnants of the party and I brought him a beer. He smiled up at me as he took it, "Why thank you Nurse Goodbody." Indeed. My body prickled with excitement.

How long had I known Mitchell? He and Glenn had been friends since high school, so he'd been in our house sharing meals, talking to our mom, teasing me since I was fourteen. Why hadn't I noticed him before? Looked at him. Considered him.

Clustered in our hippy-converted dining room around Glenn's wooly recliner and the silent TV, we passed joints and laughed. My usual spot was on the floor next to Glenn, or in the orange velvet rocker beside him, but Dave sat there now. He offered to get up, but I declined and sat on the couch across from Mitchell so I could watch him and think about the charge he'd sent through me.

When it came time to change the cassette, I took requests for music. More Lynyrd Skynyrd? Waylon and Willie? Creedence? Johnny Winter? We shifted to the blues.

Mitchell was married now, of course. So where was Darla, I wondered, looking again at his profile. Just then, he turned to look at me. No, into me. I had to draw a deep breath. I had to breathe. I drew that breath and smiled at him. I shifted, stretching, feigning fatigue, arching my back, reveling in the sensation; sharing it.

Arnold and Kathy left without my knowing. Now Dave mumbled something and got to his feet. "You going?" Glenn asked.

"Yeah. It was fun, man. I'll call you tomorrow."

Hale got up too, established his balance and headed toward the door. "See ya, H," Glenn said, somehow knowing that Hale was on his way. "Drive safe."

I got up to see them to the door and Mitchell followed. When I turned back to face him, he was close. We stood for a moment like magnets, pulsing and pulling, a force between us. Then he leaned in and kissed me, the softest, briefest kiss. "I want to see you," he said.

Oh yes, Mitchell. I want to see you too.

Maybe it's true what they say about a blind person's other senses being heightened. All I know is that somehow, Glenn already knew what was transpiring between Mitchell and me. When I slipped into my rocker next to him, he said, "Darla will kill you."

No, I didn't think so. In point of fact Darla once told me I could have Mitchell. She didn't mean it of course. She was mad about something. Disgusted. I hadn't given it much thought at the time.

But now I was thinking about it.

A couple of nights later, Mitchell came to the door late. Glenn was already hooked up to the dialysis machine. He slept as its valves clicked open and closed. Solution flowed into and drained out of his abdomen. I liked having the night to myself.

It must have been midnight when Mitchell cracked open the front door and peered across the darkened living room.

I sat in Glenn's wooly recliner in the den lit only by the TV's fluorescent glow. He stepped in and paused before striding toward me. He stood in front of me and brought out a joint and lit it, drawing long on its twisted end.

We settled onto the floor. Each time he offered me the joint pinched between his thumb and index finger, I laid my hand over his and let it rest a moment before lifting the joint from his grasp. He watched my lips when I took a hit. I smiled at him and held the smoke in my lungs inviting it to soften the world.

Soon we stretched the lengths of our bodies and lay facing each other on the shag. So now, when neither Patti Lee nor Joanne could go to Las Vegas, when Dave and Hale had to beg off, when Arnold and Kathy didn't have the money to go, it winnowed down to Glenn and Mitchell and me. I was happy and relieved to have Mitchell with us for multiple reasons, all selfish: He would help me. He would muscle the wheelchair. He would share the conversational load. He could maneuver the casino and he understood the games. I didn't care that he would leave us to fly home Sunday to work and to Darla. I would manage the last day. I'd get us home. Mitchell would look at me with his twinkling eyes. He would smile and hold me and make me believe his lies. We could all set reality aside and pretend everything was going to be okay.

Glenn and I had been up late the night before and early the morning of the flight. I had him packed and packed myself. He bathed and I showered. We ate scrambled eggs and hash browns and I gave him his shot. I moved our bags close to the front door. He put on his leg and checked the location of his cane repeatedly.

Mitchell pulled his green-and-white work truck up close to the house. He kissed me at the door and studied my face, his eyes twinkling. He held me by the waist and whispered, "Ready?" I kissed him again and our mouths opened for the warm connection.

He pushed me away but kept his eyes on mine as he called out to Glenn, "Ready?"

Glenn answered as he always did, "Born that way."

Mitchell and I lifted our luggage and Glenn's chair into the bed of the truck. With Glenn sitting shotgun, I got in on Mitchell's side, slid under the wheel and settled in with my hand on his thigh.

Glenn explained the system he had devised for pacing himself, to be sure he wouldn't run out of money before Monday. Each day, he would put a set amount in his right pocket. He'd gamble out of his right pocket only and draw more from the left the next day. That's how he'd keep track of his wins and losses.

Our little entourage turned heads at Tulsa International Airport as we checked in and trundled along the concourse toward the gate. We were seated up front in economy class and I sat between the men, arm-in-arm on both sides. Glenn seemed very proud and happy, his small smile impossible to hide.

We hired a cab at McCarran Airport and rode to the Stardust. We stood at the reception desk, checked in and rode up in the cool, mirrored elevator, then wheeled Glenn into his room and oriented him to the setup. Here's the bed, the phone, the bathroom door. I put his insulin in the mini fridge and handed him the remote control.

Then Mitchell and I left him there in his wheelchair with a question on his face. We went to our room next door and made love and napped. Glenn's Las Vegas adventure was delayed until we were satisfied one more time.

II.

Mitchell tapped on the door to Glenn's room and we waited. Not sure if I heard a groggy response, I hesitated, then used the key.

He was still in his chair. The TV was on, but the hotel's in-house channel played its continuous loop of advertisements.

Shame overtook me. I couldn't look at Mitchell and was glad in that moment that Glenn couldn't look at me.

"I thought you would nap," I said, weak, pathetic.

"No. I'm not sleepy," he said. Of course he wasn't sleepy. He had been revved up and ready to go from the moment we left Tulsa, from weeks and months before.

"Okay," I said, barely able to clear my throat. "Wanna get something to eat?"

"Sure," he said, and we headed downstairs, a grim trio.

Mitchell steered us into the first restaurant we encoun-tered on the casino floor, an elaborate diner with oversized booths, patterned carpet, and no natural light. We talked through the menu and, when the waitress paused before us, we placed our orders with only one delay. Instead of asking Glenn what he wanted, she looked away from him and then at me. "What does he want?" she whispered.

I kept my expression blank and let her question hang between us before I turned to Glenn and said, "Tell the lady what you want," and he did. Flustered, she scribbled her notes and started to walk away, but turned back to us and said, "Would you like to play some Keno while you're waiting?" Why yes, we would. "I'll send a runner."

Within moments, a runner dressed like a jockey in a silky white shirt with a large number 16 on the back left a handful of cards and pencils, and that was all it took to shift the mood. Glenn picked numbers on card after card and our meals became secondary to watching the screen above us and shouting again and again as he won three, four, five games in a row.

It was a sign. It was surely a sign.

We left the diner and stopped first at a roulette wheel. Glenn picked a number, placed his bet; the marble clicked and bounced through the smooth rotation and he won. He put nickels and quarters and dollars into slot machines and bet on jai-alai matches in Florida and won. He spun the Wheel of Fortune and it paid $40 and $40 and $250 and more.

We drew attention at each stop: The girl with the long hair and the blind man in the wheelchair who couldn't lose. Oh sure, we lost, but mostly we won. Glenn won. I stood close and pushed his hair off his forehead or rested my hand on his shoulder. Mitchell played his own hands and read Glenn's cards for him at the blackjack table, but Glenn scratched the felt and drew, or stood on his hand with a cut of the air, his fingers held straight. He doubled down and he won; all the while, he smiled a sly smile, a smile from within, a smile reflecting his knowing that this was his time, his dream, his moment.

In the eerie, unnatural half-light of the casino, time held its breath, or exhaled and rushed forward, we didn't know; we were entranced. When we shook off the spell and found a table at the edge of the sports book, we laughed and re-lived this hand or that spin or the look on that dealer's face.

Glenn had his chips in a rack now and Mitchell did too, though his winnings weren't half what Glenn had amassed. "Cash these chips for me," Glenn said, and pushed the rack across the table toward me. "I want the folding money."

I went to the cashier's window and in short order she counted out $996 then fanned it across the counter in front of me. We smiled at each other as I scooped up the bills, tapped them into a stack, folded them once and headed back to our table.

When I arrived, Glenn sat with his hand resting on his chest. I glanced at Mitchell who gave me an "I don't know" shrug.

"Hey, Money Bags, are you all right?"

He straightened himself and said, "Yeah. I guess I'm tired-er than I realized." He looked subdued. We'd been at it full tilt since we left the diner.

"Well maybe $1000 will perk you up," I said as I took his hand and transferred the folded wad of bills from my palm to his.

"A thousand?!" he grinned.

"Nine hundred and ninety-six bucks!"

"Wow! I knew I was winning, but I kinda lost track."

"How much did you have in your right pocket?"

"I started with $100," he said. "I didn't think we'd been at it that long."

It wasn't hard to convince him to call it a night, and, when we reached his room, the clock on the nightstand read 6:15. A wedge of sunlight forced its way through a gap in the blackout curtains and confirmed it was not p.m., but a.m. I put the "Do Not Disturb" placards on his doorknob and ours and we slept well into the day on Saturday, Glenn's second day since dialysis.

The casino had a lavish buffet and we headed there for our first meal of the day. We devised a plan whereby Mitchell and I would bring plates of cocktail shrimp, crab legs, prime rib, scalloped potatoes, green beans, green salads, and garlic bread. Whatever we could find, we'd bring it along with extra plates and then we'd eat at our booth, family style. Glenn's assignment was to order our drinks when the waitress came by.

"I should have peed before we left the room," I said to Mitchell. "I'll make a quick run and meet you at the buffet."

"I'll go too," Mitchell said, laughing. "Great bladders think alike!"

"Will you be alright?" I asked Glenn before we left.

"I'm fine," he said. "Rum and Coke, all around."

Mitchell and I stepped out of the confines of the buffet and wove our way through rows of slot machines and around the perimeter, past a bank of blackjack tables, beyond the sports book and cashier and finally to the restrooms. By the time we retraced our steps around the casino floor, foraged the length of the buffet's offerings, and returned to the booth, 20 minutes or more elapsed. Yet there sat Glenn, alone and drinkless.

"No drinks?" Mitchell asked.

"No, they never stopped by."

"You're kidding," I glanced at the busy and efficient wait staff bustling in and out among tables and booths all around us. Just at that moment, a young woman with red lips and a red ribbon in her hair stopped next to me and said, "Can I bring you something to drink?"

"Glenn?" I said.

"Rum and Coke all around."

She blinked and forced a smile, made a note on her pad and turned to go. We sat quietly for a moment, each replaying the affront. I stroked Glenn's shoulder. "It makes me so mad," I said.

"Yeah, me too," he replied, then paused, drew a deep breath and said, "What have we got here?"

"Prime rib!" Mitchell announced, "and lobster tail!" We dug into the feast at hand and mapped out our strategy for the day.

With full bellies and anticipation, we embarked on our game plan: Mitchell would try his hand at baccarat. Glenn and I would work the casino according to well-established gambler's lore that tables and machines most visible to the newly arrived paid the most liberally. We would work the circumference of the casino floor. We would stay at any one location no more than seven minutes if a losing pattern developed. And how would we know it was a losing pattern? Why, we'd know! We weren't going to be sentimental. We weren't going to get attached to a sympathetic dealer. No superstitious mumbo jumbo! If we lost three hands in a row, or four or five, we'd know: Time to move on!

Glenn said he put $300 in his right pocket for Saturday. And why not? He had already won ten times what he set aside for the first day! This was the dream come true. We were in it; we breathed it; we lived it.

So, when he was down $100 after seven minutes at the first roulette table to the right of the buffet, we were only mildly sobered. We had a blueprint after all. We would work it. We straightened our shoulders and pulled up our chins and moved on, not to the very first blackjack table we encountered, but the next one, or the one after that.

And with cold precision, the prim young dealer relieved us of another $100.

Okay. Let's step back. We paused adjacent to the reception desk and regrouped. Glenn still had $100 in his right pocket, but no one wants to gamble from a defensive position, right? It only works against you, like you came to lose. He pulled the folded wad of bills from his left pocket and peeled off $400. He reasoned that left him with sufficient funds for Sunday, and he was playing with his winnings! His original stake was still intact.

So we found a craps table and played even and odd and red and black and numbers and double zero. We won and lost and won again. We were a draw—the blind man, frail and haggard, and his clear-eyed companion—she of the long hair and short skirt. We were a novelty, an anomaly. People wondered about our relationship, I imagined. And

I supposed they thought lots of things except that we were sister and brother.

At last, after much ado in the spotlight, we lost three in a row and then it was seven minutes and ten minutes and half an hour into a losing streak. If we had been up a couple hundred dollars or more, we had now let all but a little of today's allowance go. Only then, demoralized, would Glenn agree to be rolled away from the table.

"I'm hungry," I said.

"Is there a Wheel of Fortune around here?"

"Glenn…"

"No, is there?"

There was. We rolled up and Glenn took his last $10 and told me to play it on the Lucky Eagle, a unique slot on the wheel that occurs only once, long odds—54 to one.

Well-oiled and exquisitely balanced, the great wheel slipped around its axis for a long, long time. Its paddle clicked against each peg, making a satisfying, rapid-fire tick, like a playing card clothes-pinned to a bicycle's fork, clattering against the spokes. Glenn cocked his head. He listened as I stood motionless and pessimistic. I watched until the wheel slowed to a rhythmic tick, then tock, tock, tock. Glenn put his hand out just before it stopped on Lucky Eagle—payout, $540.

We cashed out before dinner and Mitchell walked up right on cue, slipped his hand around my waist and kissed my ear.

Given the tenuous nature of our wins that day—and Mitchell's losses at baccarat, doubling down until his entire stash was exhausted—I broached the idea of retiring for the night. Glenn surprised me with ready compliance. The day had been stressful in its way, winning and losing until we gritted our teeth. Even the final spin of the Wheel of Fortune, in spite of the outcome, took its toll. Depleted, Glenn agreed to the retreat without resistance.

III.

Mitchell had a two o'clock flight back to Tulsa, so we slept through multiples of the snooze alarm. We were facing each other when we opened our eyes. His smile showed his pleasure in finding me there. We took our time making love, and when he went to shower, I called next door for Glenn.

No answer.

I didn't feel concerned. We'd been pushing for two full days. I'd shower and let him sleep a little longer.

Mitchell packed his bag and stood by the door. "I'll pick you up at the airport tomorrow," he said, his eyes twinkling.

We stepped into the hallway and I walked him to the elevator. When its doors slid together between us, I drew a deep breath and turned back toward Glenn's room.

I knocked on his door and waited. Hearing nothing, I used the key and went in to find him on his side, unmoving. I stopped, suspended above him.

"Hey," I said and leaned over him in the dim light. I watched for a moment to see his stomach rise and settle. He was breathing. His hair had matted to his face, so I threaded my finger under it and pushed it aside. "Hey."

He stirred.

"How are you feeling?"

"Tired," he said. Then, "A little queasy."

"Oh—let's get you some breakfast!" I called for room service, including ginger ale.

"While we wait, why don't you go ahead and have a bath?"

I arranged the soap and shampoo and filled the tub, then stepped out and let him roll into the room.

"Your stuff is on the corner near the faucet," I said and closed the door behind him. I leaned my cheek against the door and said, "Let me know if you need anything."

When I heard a gentle splash of water, I propped myself up on the bed and turned on the TV—Family Feud.

Just as our breakfast arrived on a rolling cart covered with a white tablecloth, pushed by a boy in an ill-fitting uniform, Glenn opened the bathroom door and sat bare-chested in his wheelchair, his hair dripping. The boy stopped when he saw Glenn and stared. Maybe Glenn's ghostly complexion caught him off guard. Or the fact that only one foot extended past the flared legs of his jeans. The boy had not developed the aplomb of a polished domestic.

"I'll take it from here," I said and handed him a five-dollar chip.

"Thanks," he said and looked back at Glenn before he made his exit.

I handed Glenn his shirt and said, "Let's start with something sparkly." I poured some ginger ale over ice. Glenn took the glass and sipped and sipped again. He nibbled at scrambled eggs and link sausage. He began to perk up and soon we each took big bites of halves of a toasted bagel to which I had applied cream cheese, smoked salmon, and capers.

"Did Mitchell take off?"

"Yep. He's on his way. He said he'd pick us up tomorrow."

"Great." He paused. Seemed to be taking inventory. "I think I'll go back to the bathroom."

He wheeled back where he came from and closed the door. I could hear him jostling with the chair and a decisive "clack" when he settled on the toilet. This could be a problem, I thought, and began to calculate the hours since his last dialysis. The normal break between hook-ups was 48 hours. We were now at about 65. But wait! You know what? He should be okay. This day, Sunday, should feel like any Monday after a two-day weekend break. We're good. It's okay.

As if on cue, Richard Dawson turned his back to the camera and shouted, "Survey says…!" A big red "X" flashed on the screen, accompanied by an obnoxious rasping buzzer. Wrong answer.

The toilet flushed and then silence. "You all right?" I called.

"Be a minute," was his response. He sounded strong, didn't he?

The bathroom door swung open and again my brother faced me with atrophied eyes, but upright, resolute, girded for battle. "Let's do this thing," he said, and we were out the door, down the elevator, and onto the playing field. We wove in and out among the hopefuls and those who came to lose, smokers and drinkers already fixed into position at the tables and wheels. They cranked the arms of slot machines and looked mechanical themselves.

We settled at a blackjack table and see-sawed between winning and losing until I got restless. Had it been two hours? Three? Glenn tossed a ten-dollar chip to the dealer and we rolled away from the table.

"Let's just walk," I said, and he agreed. We headed right and encountered a group of grannies, fresh off their tour bus. They cackled and chuckled and clutched their bags, excited for the day. When they saw us, they hushed and split, and we passed through the gaggle; our wake closed behind us.

I resumed my role as eyes for Glenn. "Oh!" I said, "It looks like we have newlyweds." Glenn turned his head as though he too could see. "They can't be more than 19 or 20," I said. "He's so thin! And mutton chops!" Glenn had to laugh. "His new wife looks smarter than he does," I speculated. "That could be trouble!"

Then, like bells in a fire station, an alarm sounded and a man at a one-dollar slot jumped out of his seat and threw his arms in the air. Gamblers all around turned and whooped and hollered with him. We stopped too, to participate in his win. And, yes, we were near the door.

Natural light streamed in, and I turned Glenn's chair toward it. "Let's breathe some real air," I said, and he agreed.

We rolled out through glass doors under the enormous awning that defined the casino's drive-through entrance. A valet turned toward us, and I waved him off. He watched as we rolled to the edge of shade where a concrete knee wall made a seat for me. We sat at right angles. Glenn listened and I watched as cars slipped out of the glare of the Las Vegas sun and into the artificial twilight of the overhang. Each one paused to have its doors opened, both sides at once, by officious young men.

We sat for a while without speaking, then Glenn said, "Thanks for bringing me here."

"You're paying for it," I quipped. He smiled. "Ready to get back to it?"

"Born that way."

We crossed back into the counterfeit atmosphere of the casino, and its incandescent lights, its smoky aura, closed around us. From that point forward we played systematically. We clocked into and out of our seats at blackjack tables around the edge of the floor. We won and lost and lost and won. The Wheel of Fortune shined on us or it frowned. We alternated craps and roulette, paused only for cocktail shrimp, pastrami sandwiches and fries, then right back to it. After a timeless day of determined gambling, Glenn said, "I think I'm ready to go up."

We'd been losing at the roulette wheel, a long streak of bad spins. The other gamblers—a ruddy man in a cowboy hat who played 28 and black no matter what; a couple of divorcees who bumped into each other, laughed loudly, and rested their breasts on the lip of the table; and a young man with his hair tied into a long braid down his back and turquoise rings on both hands—smiled at us and nodded as we turned to go. The croupier shook his head as though he felt remorseful or sorry for Glenn or me.

We made our way upstairs and, once in the room, Glenn said, "I'm pooped."

"Big travel day tomorrow," I said. "It's a good idea to be rested."

I don't know how he spent that last night at the Stardust, but when I went in to start the process in the morning, he had found the trash can and pulled it next to his bed. Vomit pooled in its plastic liner.

"Uh-oh," I said.

"Yep."

"Let's get this show on the road."

He sat up and I pushed his hair back, making a big forehead. He was pale and his breathing labored. He retched and I handed him the wastebasket. He sat with it on his lap and heaved a couple more times but produced nothing.

"Come on," I said. "Let's go home."

He was quiet while I busied myself packing his things. We went to the diner for a quick egg sandwich. He said he felt okay, but he sat forward in his chair with his arm just across his middle. He rode in the cab that way and when I opened his door at curbside, he leaned out and threw up on the sidewalk.

"Oh, Bubba," I said.

"Sorry," he said and wiped his mouth on his sleeve.

I paid the cabbie and we wheeled up to the desk to check into our flight, but Glenn began to retch again.

"Is he sick?" The young woman behind the counter—Brenda—looked as though she were the one with a bad taste in her mouth.

"I'm all right now," Glenn said.

She pulled her gaze from him to me and said, "We can't let him board if he's sick."

"We have tickets for the two o'clock flight and we need to get on it."

"That's it," Glenn said. "I threw up outside. There's nothing left. I won't be sick again."

She directed her next sentence to the young man at the counter to her right—Brent. "We can't let him board if he's sick," she said pointedly. Brent took a step toward her side of the counter.

"We need to get home," I said, my agitation audible behind a veneer of civility. "He's not going to be sick again. Please, just give us our boarding passes."

"Where's John?" Brenda asked.

"Lunch." Brent replied, staring at Glenn.

"Is that your supervisor?" They raised their eyes to me, and I could see they were afraid. They did not know what to do about Glenn and they were about to go bureaucratic.

"John? Good. Call him. Call John and tell him you're going to keep this man off his flight because he was sick to his stomach. He needs dialysis. In Tulsa. It's set up and waiting for him. And if you keep him here, if you don't let us get home in time, you will be responsible for what happens to him without it!" I pointed my finger at Brent and then Brenda.

They stood motionless, stunned. Travelers nearby grew quiet and waited. I guess I had gotten loud.

"Well?"

"Go ahead," Brent said under his breath. "Let 'em go."

He moved back to his station. Brenda fumbled with our paperwork and made no eye contact when she handed it over. I took the passes with shaking hands and a terse "Thank you." We made our way to the gate and boarded the plane as though we held carte blanche.

The flight seemed interminable. Glenn leaned against the small plastic window for the duration, not asleep, but not awake. I marveled at my own assertiveness, and the quaking in my chest subsided as panicky images of unfamiliar hospital ERs, quagmires of questions, and frightful delays receded with the hot Las Vegas sand.

Mitchell met us and we navigated the airport exit, the freeway across town, Sheridan to Florence Avenue, up the crumbling driveway, into the house and down the hall to Glenn's room, where heavy cases of dialysate waited. Glenn fell onto his bed and surrendered, almost 100 hours since his last peritoneal flush.

Mitchell stood in the doorway while I set up the machine. I knew the steps by rote and ticked them off rhythmically. The process complete, I released the clamp on the tube to Glenn's belly and the clear fluid started to flow.

I turned to look, but Mitchell was gone.

At the other end of the hallway in my room, I fell onto my own bed, and Glenn and I slept.

IV.

A sound pulls me from concentrated sleep. What is that? Buzzing. Rasping. I force my eyes open. I'm rigid, in deep sleep, on my back with arms at my sides and fists clenched, teeth grinding. What am I hearing?

I lift my head, just a tilt, to see past the end of the bed, between my feet to the hallway. Then a light. A glow really. Faint. Movement. What is that? Is someone there? "Glenn?"

He rises up from the foot of the bed. The top of his head. He looks down at something. Now his shoulders come into view. What? His hair looks black. And he rises, his arms opening wide. A cape?! Wings. He lifts his face to me now and his blind eyes burn, white. His mouth opens in a ghastly grin, sharp teeth, blood running red, dark red down his chin. Buzzing. Rasping. Louder, louder. Screeching.

I am frozen, paralyzed, locked here on my back. Frantically I push into the mattress, my own eyes wide, my own teeth bared in terror.

And then, BANG! I'm awake. Glenn's dialysis machine squalls. It's the alarm. So loud. Incessant. The line is kinked again. Or the reservoir is dry. Maybe he rolled over and pulled it out of level.

Like a reanimated corpse in a horror movie, my skeleton forces itself up, awkwardly, disjointedly, until, at last, fluid movement is restored. I make my way down the hall with waves of fear pulsing up my spine until I flip on the light. The vampire is vanquished and Glenn and I both grimace and squint at the stab of light.

"How long?" I ask.

"Not sure," he says, putting his forearm over his eyes.

Wait. Can he see? Is the light hurting his eyes?

"Glenn?" I say and lean toward him when he sweeps his arm out wide and again, his blind eyes spring open, white and blazing and his teeth are bare. He lunges for me and I jerk backward, convulsing to avoid his grasp.

With that, I am truly awake, my chest heaving. The dialysis machine's alarm screams like a siren; it approaches and retreats, the infernal hum swells and recoils as I move down the hall, turn on the light and flip the switch to shut the machine up.

"Hey," Glenn says to me. My heart throbs, my breath is shallow. I clear my throat, but still can only croak. "Hey, Bubba."

Chapter Twenty-Five

Herr Fronkenstein & Frau Blücher

He'd had a rough night. Then, the alarm on his dialysis machine blasted at exactly 2:00 a.m., sending him into a cramp and a grimace. It jerked me straight up and out of my bed.

I came down the hall barefoot in my oversized OU T-shirt and flipped on the light in his room; the yellow glare gave me a grimace to match his. I shut off the alarm and, as the blaring noise made its retreat, I surveyed our situation. Glenn lay angled across his bed with the sheets twisted to the side. His fine hair was tangled, his lips pressed into a firm line of determination against the pain. The carousel of heavy glass two-liter dialysate bottles stood on the rolling rack next to his bed; the bottles hung bottoms up, each with a tube that ran to the distribution box below. I stood there in my nightshirt, sleep relegated to the back of the line.

"How ya doin'?" I asked. Our routine.

"Great," he shifted his lower body. "You?"

"Great as well."

"I'm pretty full," he said, and ran his waxen fingers across his belly, distended with fluid.

"Velly eentelesting," I said, and he struggled to smile.

According to peritoneal dialysis troubleshooting protocol, I started at the top of the rack and traced the process. It looked like three of the six bottles had drained through him and into the disposal bag on the floor. The fourth bottle had emptied all but a small pool of solution collected in its funneled end. The clear liquid wobbled in place when I tilted the bottle, but otherwise lay motionless. "Okay, we're blocked somewhere." I ran my fingers down the clear plastic channel to his abdomen and discovered a white fibrous mass had collected in the tube just above the hole into his stomach wall. Not good.

I prepared a syringe full of Heparin and injected it to dissolve the obstruction. Reminded as always of Gene Wilder in *Young Frankenstein*, I checked the distribution box. It could have been a creature assembled by that mad scientist, with rivets on the outside of its seams and two simple phony-looking gauges offering information about the pressure and flow of the liquid. They seemed fine.

"How's it look?" Glenn asked.

"We're good now upstream. Let's see why you're not draining."

Below the box, another tube connected to the disposal bag on the floor below. It had curled onto itself and kinked. I clamped it off close to the box and disconnected it from the bag. It took only a few seconds for the hose to relax and release the kink. I smoothed it and smoothed it again. I relocated the bag to require a longer stretch from the box above, reconnected the hose, and removed the clamp.

The fluid in his abdomen began to drain freely. Within a moment or two, he felt relief from the pressure.

"Good job, Frau Blücher," he said.

"My pleasure, Herr Fronkenstein." I smoothed his hair away from his forehead. "Need anything else?"

"Nope. Let's call it a night."

"Good night, then."

I flipped the light switch and padded back down the hallway to my bed.

Chapter Twenty-six

Out of His Body

Glenn said he couldn't remember what I looked like. I told him not to worry. As long as he could remember Christie Brinkley, he could remember me.

He gave me a wry look, but I could see the realization distressed him. He'd been blind long enough that he could no longer remember my face, or mom's face. He told me one evening when we'd both smoked enough pot to cloud the room and blot out all but the one thought.

I could only think of the maudlin old movie, *A Patch of Blue*, and Glenn's sad and profound revelation.

"My eyes have shrunk," he said. He put his hand up and touched his eyelids. They had. Atrophy. But I could not bring myself to confirm it.

"No," I said. "No, I don't think so." Then, "It doesn't matter," I said, though I knew my platitude was no help. He didn't answer.

***

Our cousins and his friends visited him almost every day, on their way to work or their way home, on their lunch hours, evenings. We sat in a semi-circle around the TV with Glenn in the middle. We passed joints and watched OU beat Texas. We shouted at the screen and died and lived with the Sooners.

I think Glenn liked to watch football most because the announcers told him what was happening on the screen. The rest of the time, his imagination had to suffice.

I enrolled at the University of Tulsa and picked up where I left off from UC Santa Barbara. Mornings I would get breakfast together, give him his shot, and head off to class.

For months he got dressed, including his leg, which meant shoes too, and walked his Walter Brennan walk down the narrow hallway from his bedroom at the back of the house. He ran his fingertips along the rough plastered wall as he went. First, he passed the door into the kitchen, then crossed the poster-sized grate of the floor furnace before he reached the door into the dining room we used as a den.

He paused there and rested his palm on the doorframe to ensure a stable turn. The TV sat just left of the door, so he gripped the frame, leaned across to find the knob and pull it to turn on the set. Then he straightened up, steadied himself, and counted the last four steps to his chair. Here he would walk the blind man's walk with his hand extended at an angle in front of him, even though he knew his toe would reach the chair first.

Squared up in front of the chair, he put his right hand on the opposite armrest, swiveled on his heel and transferred his weight; he buckled his knees and fell back into the seat. Safe.

The phone and the cable box at his side, he passed the mornings in daytime drama and reverie. That's where I'd find him when I came home after morning classes. Sometimes he'd be asleep, pushed back to level in the wooly chair, Waylon tucked in between his leg and the chair's oversized arm. Other times he'd call out as soon as I opened the door.

"Quick! Come here and tell me what's happening!"

I'd dash to his side and look at the screen. A scoundrel on *Days of Our Lives* seemed to be scheming against her rival. She moved about the scene surreptitiously. She placed clues to an imaginary affair, planted suspicion in the mind of a trusting dupe: lipstick on a wine glass, a phone number on crumpled paper. She looked satisfied in an unsavory way. She was securing her place in her lover's heart.

That was the best I could do.

"I wondered," he would say. "She was talking to her friend, and then it just got quiet for a long time."

But, before too long, Glenn quit putting his leg on just to travel the hallway and sit in his chair. He'd come down the hall on his crutches, the left leg of his bell-bottoms limp and airy below.

***

He didn't tell me everything. Maybe he fell when I wasn't home. I don't know. But the crutches and blindness proved too much to manage. Now, after I left for class, he traveled the hall on his hands and knees. We had a wheelchair, but the narrow doorways of our little old house wouldn't accommodate it.

He stopped, as always, when he turned into the dining room to pull the knob and start the TV for the day. One morning, he crawled the last few feet to his chair and nausea set in. He felt for and found the plastic trash can we'd put next to his chair, dragged it close, and vomited for the first time.

He sat back on his haunches, wiped his lips, and waited to see if that was all. Waylon came into the room and leaned into Glenn's hand. Glenn stroked the cat, pulled on his twisted tail like always. Waylon chirped his funny purring chirp and switched back and forth, drawing his body along Glenn's folded leg.

Glenn assessed his nausea, decided he was good to get into his recliner, set the can aside, rocked forward onto his knees, and grabbed the arms of the chair. Just then, his stomach convulsed again and more vomit surged into his throat. He folded back onto his haunches but when he reached for the bucket, he hit Waylon. The cat jumped and skittered, knocked the plastic trashcan onto its side. Foul liquid seeped onto the shag carpet.

And Glenn threw up over it all.

At last he felt sure he was done for a time. He stood the trashcan upright and the new vomit slid down its side. The phone began to ring. He reached for it and knocked its handset off the side table and out of reach. For a few moments he could hear the caller's voice, "Glenn? Glenn?" but when he tried again to reach it, he knocked the trashcan over again. The voice stopped with a click, and the rapid pulse of a high-pitched dial-tone set in.

He pressed his lips together hard, making a straight line, and leaned forward, putting his forehead on the seat of his chair. Tears rose to his eyes, but he drew breath after breath and refused to let them fall. At last the phone went silent.

He rested there a moment and formed his plan of action: he located the trashcan with an outstretched hand, crawled around it and into the kitchen. He pulled himself up to the sink and balanced there on his right foot, leaned against the counter before he found the faucet and let the cool water rinse his hands. He filled his cupped palms and splashed his face time after time not caring about his hair or his shirt. He put his face to the flow and drank.

Finally, he dried himself with the tea towel and rested a moment more. Then he dropped the tea towel into the sink and ran water over it, twisted it, and threw it across his shoulder. He lowered himself back down to his hands and knees and made his way back to the mess.

He wiped the outside of the trashcan as best he could, careful to not spill any of the remaining contents. He folded the towel over itself and scrubbed the thick pile of the carpet. He knew he'd found the right spot by the cool ooze collected there.

At last, certain he'd left more to do, but spent, he said he only hoped he hadn't made a worse mess. He tossed the towel toward the kitchen, heard it land on the fake-brick linoleum, a small victory. He climbed into his chair and sagged back into its wooly cushion.

Only then did he realize that the TV was on. It was on the station where they'd left it last night, he and Dave and Mitchell, a channel that, after hours, reverted to paid programming, which was still running now. A huckster prattled on about the miracle of stain removal that could be his. Exhausted, Glenn let it go for a while. But soon he was ready for a change.

He reached for the cable box. It did not sit in its customary spot on the side table. He felt for it gently, encountered a glass whose weight indicated it was not empty. He steadied the glass and continued his search. He moved his hand across the tabletop as he had moved it across his belly the night before.

A paper plate with residue of onion dip and potato chips sat close.

And nothing else.

He leaned a bit to feel the shelf below. Phone book. Cassettes. No cable box.

He pushed forward and sat on the edge of his seat, then eased down onto the floor with his back against the recliner. He leaned to the side to feel the floor under the table. The phone. He positioned the handset back into the cradle and situated it on the tabletop.

He felt again. Flip-flops. Another tea towel. Notebook paper. Nothing.

"Jim, this is the most fantastic cleanser I've ever used! Is it safe on delicate fabrics?"

"Is it ever! You can trust this new formula..." The TV front man and his shill were relentless. Happy. Loud. Incessant.

Glenn moved the trashcan and its contents toward my chair. He leaned across the front of his side table and stretched his hand back as far as it would go, holding his breath. His fingertips touched something. Nope. A paperback. A couple of pencils.

"Where can we find this miracle product, Jim?"

Glenn felt his chest tighten and his breathing become forced, measured out in swift surges. Again he compressed his lips and turned his face to the ceiling. "*No, no, no,*" he thought, shaking his head. His frustration multiplied, swelled. "*I'm fucking blind!*" he thought. "*I'm sick. I've lost everything… I just want to watch some fucking daytime TV.*"

Tears coursed into his atrophied eyes. His teeth ground across each other and he screamed, "No! No! No!"

And then he was weightless. He left his body.

He floated.

In an instant, he zipped up to the ceiling and gained an aerial view of the room from above his wooly recliner.

A view! A view! He had a VIEW!

He could see.

He could see the room and his chair, the top of his own head, Waylon near the door licking a curled-up paw, the TV. He saw the couch with its rumpled slipcover. He saw last night's roaches in the ashtray and glasses with the brown liquid of Coke settled to the bottom and the clear liquid of melted ice suspended on top.

And then, he saw the cable box. On the floor in front of the couch. That's right. Dave had it there last night.

He snapped back into himself and sat dumbfounded, blind again. In that surreal moment he leaned forward crawled across to the couch, put his hand on the cable box. He sat with it there for another moment before he turned and brought it back to his chair.

He didn't change the channel for a while, but sat instead at the edge of his recliner, both hands resting on the box. He replayed his experience once, twice, and again. "I was looking down from above," he marveled. "I could see my-self...I could see."

At last, with an astonished shake of his head, he pushed himself back, reclined, and slept.

Chapter Twenty-Seven

Glenn Asks Me

The day Glenn asked me to end his life, we were both high. Maybe we had been into that premium Oaxacan—something potent. We sat side-by-side, he in his wooly recliner and I in my orange plush-velvet rocker. Mork & Mindy engaged in an animated faux argument on the TV screen, but the sound was muted and, of course, Glenn couldn't see them anyway.

We'd had Taco Bell for dinner—again—and now, at high volume, Eric Clapton laid out a strategy for getting through the night, "If you want to get down, down on the ground, cocaine." Our brains throbbed on the wavelength of the bassline and had set aside deep thought and polite conversation. Or at least mine had. At best, staring at the TV screen, I might have been thinking about Pam Dawber and Robin Williams. Was the chemistry real? Were they an item?

When I glanced left and saw that Glenn was talking to me, I had to grab a mental tether, and, hand over hand, haul my mind back to the here-and-now. I willed myself toward him from across a great foggy distance. Mork & Mindy shrank away, and I felt drawn in reverse from a place of heavy insulation, back into my body and my orange plush chair.

"I'm just so tired," he was saying, his voice just audible.

I straightened myself and leaned toward him, squinted, concentrated. Clapton interjected: "She don't lie, she don't lie, she don't lie, cocaine."

"Wait a minute!" I shouted and lurched out of the rocker toward the stereo to turn the volume down. I pivoted and returned to my seat, secured a lucky landing, and assumed the posture of a proper caregiver, upright, alert, Clapton only a faint, etheric thread now, "Would you know my name if I saw you in Heaven?"

Glenn had been declining, there was no denying it. Since Las Vegas, the dialysis no longer refreshed him as it had. He felt sick soon after each session. His doctors prescribed Phenergan for his nausea and vomiting, and I became adept at snapping the tops off those glass ampules and injecting this latest intramuscular medication deep to stave off the effects of his persistently toxic system.

Edema troubled him, and he developed neuropathy even in his phantom leg. Miasma and fatigue dulled his curiosity and sharp wit. Respites became brief and exceptional. Diarrhea set in—recurrent, explosive—accompanied by roiling cramps. The hallway to the bathroom stretched long when you traveled on your hands and knees.

A few nights before, I overheard him talking to Dave. They huddled together in Glenn's bedroom at the end of the hall. Just a snippet caught my ear as I passed toward the kitchen, "Carolyn'll do it."

I did not reroute myself and join them to find out what he was volunteering me for. I figured I would find out soon enough. He could not do much of anything for himself, so what else was he supposed to do? He relied on me.

Maybe I had come through the front door after classes just in time to hear him on the phone, "My sister will pick it up." And I would go right back out to the library for the latest books-on-tape, even though he didn't care about them.

He was so excited when we got a CB radio installed in the Porsche. He had a base unit on the table next to the phone so he could always find me, always be in touch, always apprise me of his wants and needs.

Or I might already be at the pharmacy refilling his prescriptions when the phone would ring behind the counter. With the receiver at her ear, the tech would turn and look in my direction, "Are you Carolyn?" she would ask. "Your brother says you're out of Cokes..." A pause, listening, "and Doritos."

And now, here, with the undercurrent of Clapton thrumming and my senses in a standoff for dominance over the Oaxacan, Glenn was telling me what he wanted. He wanted this whole thing to be over. Even Taco Bell didn't taste right anymore, and his friends didn't know what to say or do. He was too preoccupied with his sickness and pain to make them laugh. He did not want to get up another day to vomit, to soil himself, to anticipate only more and more and more of that.

It would not be hard, he said. *I would be helping him, he said. We had everything we needed right there in the house.*

I knew I could not do it. Could not hear it. My mind reeled; I leaned over the upholstered arm of the orange velvet rocker and saw the floor open up beneath me. And there was Hell, burning bright with glowing embers, radiant heat pulsing. No, I cannot.

No, I won't. No, no, no, don't ask me. I had my hands over my ears and maybe I was screaming. I don't know, but when I stopped shaking my head Glenn was saying, "Okay. It's okay. I'm sorry. I won't ask you again."

I fell back from the precipice and he also leaned back in his chair. He pushed back on the arms but did not recline, only put his head back and tilted his chin upwards. He closed his eyes and he took deep breaths, steeling himself, recalculating his future.

At last I told him I was going to bed. He held out his hand to me and I took it. We sat like that for a long while and only broke the connection after some shame and tears and forgiveness.

Next day we resumed our routine, though Glenn quit getting out of bed every day. His bedroom was next to the bathroom, after all. When he did get up, though, he mustered a good front, welcomed his friends, watched football, and cracked some jokes. Things felt okay, if tentative, subject to quick shifts in his confidence. If a wave of cramps overtook him, he just said, "I have to go." And when he did, the house emptied— his pals gathered their paraphernalia, shook their heads with sadness, made sheepish eye contact, and took their leave—the particulars abandoned to the two of us who were so familiar.

Chapter Twenty-Eight

The Red Balloon

Glenn's decline had been a long one. We didn't recognize its early milestones as markers on that road. During high school, he wet the bed and it smelled sweet. Years passed. He lost his leg. More years. Then his eyes clouded. From there, the pace of the progression picked up. Surgeries, blindness. Neuropathy. Edema. Pneumonia.

Pneumonia again. Kidney failure. Dialysis…

When I left California and came home to live with Glenn, he needed me. He was blind and without his leg. He sold Glenn's Coney Island without nostalgia or sentiment and settled into his wooly recliner.

Vision Services came to call making sure Glenn knew the benefits available to him. He had been a successful small business owner. He did that without his leg, but without his eyes, no.

When I got to Tulsa, Glenn and I immediately began to talk about his death. He wanted everything in place, not to leave me with sad work. The house went into my name. We sold his van and smoked the proceeds. His lap steel went to Terry and the Turkey Mountain Troubadours.

On the day he died, I came home to find him asleep in his wooly recliner, Waylon nestled along his thigh. Glenn's hand rested on the cat's back. Waylon raised his head at my entrance; he stared at me and blinked before lowering his chin back onto his paws.

Glenn drew slow breaths, and each exhale was short and hard. I moved around the room without a sound, watching him as I went. I folded the blanket on the couch. He didn't wake. I took dishes to the kitchen and set them in the sink. When I leaned over him to feel his forehead and pet the cat, I saw it there at the bottom of his trashcan: a needle and syringe. Nothing else. Dave had been here. They had done it. Glenn would not wake up today and make me laugh.

I sat across from him in the angled light of the afternoon. He was motionless but for his breathing. Now his mouth popped open with each shallow inhale and closed again like a fish drawing water through its gills. He did not struggle, and I only waited. The time between breaths grew longer and longer. At last he stopped.

But then again his mouth opened and closed, open and closed.

And then it did not open.

We sat together in the still afternoon. Next door I heard a car door and a woman's voice. A song sparrow chirped, flittered across the porch. Waylon stood and stretched; he arched his back and shivered before he hopped down and left the room. I heard him crunching his kibble in the kitchen.

At last I went to Glenn and smoothed his fine, wavy hair, making sure he had a big forehead. I brought the manicure kit and clipped his nails, placing his hands in his lap. I straightened his shirt collar and sleeves. Then I put the blanket over his legs and moved his hands to the top.

Watching him, I remembered the hypnotic regression he had asked me to lead him through some weeks before. He was thinking of death that day, or of crossing the threshold.

He never evinced fear, but he felt unsure. Glenn wondered, like we all do, not so much what it is like to be dead, but, as George Carlin put it, what it's like to get dead.

It was guided visualization, really. Not true hypnosis. I had participated in it dozens of times myself. Total relaxation and direction to focus.

Take a deep breath and, step by step, starting with your toes and the soles of your feet, just relax. Feel the warmth. Feel the blood flow. Now up to your ankles and even your shins, and into your calf muscles, just relax.

I wondered at this point if Glenn felt awkward, since he had only one foot, one ankle, one calf. But I pressed on.

Feel your body settle and your knees relax.

He had two knees and, from there on, no other distractions. I told him to notice his thighs, his pelvis and his hips relaxing.

Tension just draining away. Completely relaxed.

I led him through a thorough relaxation up to the muscles of his face and even his scalp.

Just breathe deeply and relax.

And now you see yourself standing at the edge of a meadow. The sun is warm and the grass is green. It shifts gently in the soft breeze. And you see a pathway in front of you.

You walk along the path now in the sun on a beautiful day and you remember you have a question. Something you'd like to know. Say the question in your mind.

As you remember your question, up ahead you see a book on a stand, waiting there for you. You approach the book to find it has your question written on the cover. Read the question. Run your fingers across the words.

Take a deep breath and relax with the book in your hands. You know this book will take you to an answer. It will give you insights and understanding of your question. Maybe there are words in the book; maybe there are pictures or sounds. There may be a movie, or a feeling, or all these things. Take another deep breath and repeat your question.

Now open the book.

Glenn seemed disappointed that day. I guess he had hoped for something literal or dramatic. He said he only saw a red balloon with a string attached. It drifted upward, he said, and, caught by a breeze, it traveled higher and farther away.

I pictured the balloon floating upward from a beautiful canyon with orange cliffs and a green valley floor. Its flight gentle and easy. Glenn didn't seem to make the connection between the balloon and the soul's release from the body.

I don't know why I didn't try to explain.

But sitting there with him on the day when his breathing stopped, with the sun bronzing the air, I tried to visualize him, his spirit, his self, drifting easily upward, free of his frail, ravaged body.

No more blindness, no more vomit. Only light and flight and freedom.

Dawn.

But not the very next day.

The very next day I planned a memorial service for Glenn. I went back to Moore's Funeral Home and defied the practiced guidance of the retailer who did his best to shepherd me through the showroom circuit according to the "death care" industry's strategic plan. To his dismay, I found the least expensive casket, a plain wooden one, in a poorly lit corner, and bought it. No frills. No whistles. No bells. Perfect. I knew Glenn would be proud of me for this.

I gave the unctuous salesman Glenn's Levi's with the rabbit pelts sewn into the seams, his favorite Grateful Dead T-shirt, and one of the good-looking Pendleton shirts I'd given him for Christmas. I put an envelope labeled "green Hawaiian sand" in the man's moist hand and directed him to make sure he placed it in the casket with Glenn. He nodded and said, "Of course."

Dave came and Hale and Mitchell and others. Someone must have said something during the service, but I don't know any of that now. Surely we played Free Bird—"If I leave here tomorrow / Would you still remember me? / For I must be traveling on now / 'Cause there's too many places I've got to see."

His casket was closed. I buried him next to Mom and had a matching bronze marker engraved with his name, the dates of his birth and death, and, where hers said, "Beloved

Mother and Sister," his said, "Colonel Coney." He would have liked that, too.

Daddy was in Dubai. It hadn't occurred to me that he might want to come to Glenn's funeral.

Maybe it was the very next day after that when I pulled the madras tablecloth down from the window surrounding the air conditioner in our hippy den. I tugged at the corner until the first tack snapped free. Dust arced above me with each muffled pop as I worked my way around the window's perimeter. At one point, the cloth tore and a swatch of ragged fabric hung around the tack. I worked it loose and began again. The remainder let go with little resistance.

Behind the cloth, layers of newspaper stood fragile and stiff, and behind the papers, the aluminum foil Glenn had pressed into place against the glass was itself now rigid but unresistant.

The north-facing window, laced on the outside with cobwebs and tendrils of morning glory, let in muted light. I turned the orange velvet rocker toward it and sat looking out at the cool afternoon. With nothing in particular in my thoughts, a wisp of stress curled upward and away and diffused in the stillness there. I sat there many days. There went my mother, my marriage, my brother, and my dad, far away in Dubai.

Glenn and I had been more hunkered down than I had recognized. Holed up. Insulated. In the weeks and months that followed his funeral, I worked my way around the interior of the house, cleared clutter, vacuumed corners, let in light. Social Services came for the Books on Tape contraption and their hodgepodge of cassettes. Hillcrest retrieved his dialysis machine and cases of unused dialysate, boxes of needles and syringes and insulin out of the fridge. They collected his heparin and Imodium and glass ampules of Phenergan. They took so many boxes of cotton swabs and thermometers, though I still have a few to this day.

Did Hale take the wooly recliner? Most likely. The orange velvet rocker and floral velvet couch made their way to Goodwill. I peeled away the umber-smeared aluminum foil from my bedroom walls and painted every room in the house. Under the shag carpet and its crumbling pad lay the original, narrow-planked oak floors. I had them sanded and refinished to a satiny, honeyed glow before I brought in a new tan sofa and loveseat. I put down a circular rug from Dubai.

Sometimes, I sat alone in the evening, closed my eyes, and tried to follow the story on *M*A*S*H* or *All in the Family* by the dialogue alone. Or, of a morning, I would memorize where the eggs and bacon and hash browns and toast were on my plate, then try to eat breakfast without looking. Those experiments never lasted long. A few seconds. I did not crawl down the hallway on my hands and knees.

Glenn's buddies checked on me for a while, but that trailed off. Mitchell and I carried on until he did what married guys do—go back to their wives. I cried and cried. Then, when a little voice asked how long I would cry, I lifted my head and moved on.

Chapter Twenty-Nine

Through Daddy's Eyes

Glenn had slept hard in the mornings. Long hours through the night cycling on the dialysis machine—pumping and draining—gave way to deep, deep escape.

From my bed at the end of the hall, I could hear the surge and sigh of the contraption. Sometimes it lulled me. Sometimes I got up and puttered around to its rhythm and Glenn's sleep, straightened the house, cleaned the litter box. But this quiet morning, though Glenn was now gone and I was alone in the house, it felt as if he were still there sleeping.

I stretched to my full length, gazed upward, and played back our time together: Nights of dialysis, days of vomiting and Phenergan. Willie Nelson, Lynyrd Skynyrd. Taco Bell and Taco Bell. Marijuana, cocaine, and LSD. Escape, escape, escape.

I thought about Glenn's life, all the things he had done, and his great dignity. He survived a father who didn't want him and the death of his surrogate, our grandfather. He saw through a facile stepfather. He rose above a mean and demeaning assault. He bested the loss of his leg and established and succeeded with his own business. He lifted his head with magnanimity when his wife, Donna, left.

Even though our dad was indifferent to him, Glenn lived. But why was our dad indifferent? How could he be? And neglectful! Distant.

With these questions in my mind, I began to walk myself through the process.

I took a deep breath and, step-by-step, starting with my toes and the soles of my feet, I relaxed. Feeling the blood flow. Up to my ankles and my shins, and into my calf muscles, I relaxed.

I felt my body settle and my knees relax. Tension draining away. Completely relaxed. I relaxed the muscles of my face and even my scalp. I relaxed my jaw. Breathing deeply and relaxing.

And now I could see myself standing at the edge of a meadow. The sun was warm and the grass was green, gently moving in the soft breeze. And I saw a pathway in front of me. I walked along the path in the sun on a beautiful day and I remembered I had a question. Something I wanted to know. I said the question in my mind. As I repeated my question, up ahead I saw a book on a stand, waiting there for me.

I approached the book to find it had my question written on the cover. I read the question. I ran my fingers across the words. I took another deep breath and relaxed with the book in my hands. I knew this book would take me to an answer. It would give me insights and understanding of my question. Maybe there would be words in the book, maybe pictures or sounds. There could be a movie, or a feeling, or all these things. I opened the book...

I'm in the kitchen of our first family home, sitting at the table. No, my dad is at the table and I'm looking through his eyes. I am in my dad's head looking out, seeing with his eyes.

My mom is at the stove with her back to us, and my dad is at the table looking at a baby boy in a highchair. I can see through his eyes. It's Glenn. He's looking at Glenn.

But Glenn doesn't look right. He doesn't look right to my dad. I can see what my dad sees and baby Glenn doesn't look right to him. His skin is brown or olive, or his nose is wrong, or something. Something is wrong and my dad is disgusted. I can taste it in his mouth. This is not his son, and he is repulsed.

***

After Glenn died, it seemed like all the people who had kept that secret couldn't wait to tell it to me. My mother wasn't just pregnant with Glenn when she married my dad; Glenn was not my dad's son.

Teetum came to me first.

"About Glenn," she said, ever cryptic. "We never did care whose baby he was. We loved him just the same."

We were sitting on the floral velvet couch in the living room on Florence Avenue, her knees angling toward mine. Glenn's body was at the funeral home. The services were set for Friday.

"He looks just like his daddy," she went on. "Your momma didn't want us to say anything, so we never did. It didn't matter anyway. His daddy's the diabetic one, so you don't have to worry about that."

She was saying my brother was not my brother, but my half-brother. He was not adopted, as Glenn himself had reasoned out. Daddy never could quite bring himself to take Glenn on as his own. He was only 23, and his young wife's secret came out in Glenn's olive skin and button nose. Was there redemption for him in the fact that, so many years later, he adopted Willie, gave him his name, raised him as a son?

Somehow now, it seemed important for Teetum to tell me. She wanted me to know. Or she just couldn't hold the secret any longer. My mom, her sister, was gone. *Now Glenn is gone. Just let the secret out. Let it out. Tell Carolyn.*

Tell her that, through the years, they'd all been watching us, knowing. My mom, my dad, my aunts and uncles. Maybe they wondered if we somehow knew, Glenn and me. Maybe they looked for signs and speculated after hours on their backs in bed, talking to the darkness. Did Momma hold her breath when he asked about his button nose?

Glenn knew. More than once he poked around the subject. He told me he thought he was adopted. He tried to understand Daddy's distance and disdain. He was onto something, but no one told him the truth. Wouldn't that have been kinder?

Glenn had not mentioned it for years. He seemed to have laid it to rest. Why would I broach the subject? Now I knew, but I did not struggle with it. In that sense, Teetum was right. It did not matter anyway. It was too late. Just like all the rest, I told no one. It was my secret now too. Glenn was my brother, the end.

My dad came to me next to say that Glenn was not his son. I told him I already knew. He wanted to know how, so I told him about that morning at the breakfast table before I was born, how I looked through his eyes. Thinking I could never explain the hypnotic regression, I told him I saw it in a dream, but he did not believe me. He berated Sheila for not keeping her mouth shut. I didn't argue. My story was too fantastic to defend.

***

So…they wanted *me* to know the truth. Why? Why not Glenn? He's the one who felt the sting and needed to understand. He's the one who held his head up and pressed on into the world. Why tell me?

Chapter Thirty

Daddy, Dubai & the Dream

I never knew women did the things Molly did.

First of all, she owned her own business. An employment agency. Built on the cheap, commissioned labor of young women like me, I now understand. But it was exciting for the brief moment I worked there, making cold calls and drumming up business for her.

Molly loved opera, Italian opera, so the other girls and I listened to Mario Lanza and carried our fresh prospects along matted paths in green shag carpet from our flimsy paneled cubicles to her office. She sat behind a big desk with a lit cigarette, a Virginia Slim, held high between her shapely fingers, close to her polished nails, filed to points, just so.

Molly closed the deals, collected the fees, and calculated our commissions using a fuzzy formula of her own device. I quickly fell into arrears with my bills at home and had to call Grandma and ask her to ask Daddy if I could borrow some money. She kept his Corvette in her garage in Pawnee, managed his state-side bank account while he was in Dubai, and paid the rent for his hangar space at Harvey Young Airport. After a short wait, she sent me $600. I learned later that she had asked Daddy, "How long do you want me to keep her going?"

Sometimes, Molly would call us into her office, light up a joint, pass it, and encourage us to talk, to tell stories. Once, she wanted us to tell the most embarrassing thing about ourselves or a thing we'd done that we wished we hadn't. She got us started by telling about the time she had sex with the paper boy while her children, an infant and toddler, were asleep in another room. She didn't get caught. No harm done. But she always felt bad about it anyway, so she said.

So the stories that day were sex stories, and mousy little Annie revealed her hit-and-miss affair with a married man, a man from her church, and how they did it in his car at night in the Safeway parking lot after he dropped off his wife for the late shift.

As we laughed, and passed the joint, and took turns around the circle, I started to think about the time I got into some heavy petting with Gerald Hanson when Glenn was in the room.

Glenn was blind and Willie Nelson was turned up loud and all three of us were pretty loaded. Gerald was a great kisser and we both got excited in a hurry. The tempo accelerated and we began to peel each other's clothes off. So when Hale knocked as he opened the front door and stepped into the room, Gerald and I were nearly bare-chested. Maybe I saw Hale a split second before he turned his head in our direction. I grabbed my shirt, leapt to my feet and loped down the hall to assemble myself.

When I came back into the room wearing my best air of nonchalance, Gerald's shirt was on but unbuttoned—and Hale had unwrapped a taco for Glenn. Maybe only I felt the charge in the atmosphere. Glenn did not know, and if Gerald and Hale smiled sly smiles at their knowledge, they did it with faces averted from me, gentlemen that they were.

I blinked to find Molly and the girls staring at me. "Your turn," Molly challenged. But I felt ashamed of myself and said that I preferred not to tell. Molly let smoke from the joint drift into her eye. She squinted and said I was chickenshit, and the room grew quiet, a stratum of pot smoke suspended just above our heads.

Then her phone jangled. She picked up and listened for a moment, then looked at me with disgust and held out the receiver. "It's for you."

I stood up to take the call. It was Sheila, calling from Dubai. I tried to concentrate.

"Carolyn, your dad has died."

"What?"

"He's had a heart attack. Two in two days. He died this morning," she said from so, so far away. From Dubai. Around the world.

I recognized her voice, but... "Are you sure?" I said.

"Yes, I'm sure. That's why I'm calling. We will make the arrangements to send him home. I'll call you back when I have details."

A familiar, hollow, nothing-you-can-do-about-it sensation settled into my gut as I went about the tasks of the following days. I called Willie in Kansas and Grandma in Pawnee. Grandma! Your son, your sun, your only boy has died.

I called Teetum and, ever astute, she said, "You're an orphan now." I was. A motherless, fatherless, brotherless orphan, alone on the planet. Except for Grandma, my only grandma! And Willie. Thank God for Willie.

In the weeks and months that followed, Willie rose in my estimation from pesky little step-brother to full-on brother. He stood by me at every turn. Soon enough, Brett and Chris, half-brothers almost 20 years my junior, would rise to the title of real, true brothers too. And I would move from the protected status of Glenn's baby sister into the elevated station of big sister to Brett and Chris and Willie. And they became the scraps of family I would cling to in the ocean of emotion that followed.

***

They shipped Daddy around the world, from Dubai straight to Moore's Funeral Home. Willie and I found him in a beige room with drapes on a wall that had no window. The faintest Muzak seeped in. We stood in the chilled air, staring at the casket, sealed in the Middle East for the long ride home.

This would be the extent of our viewing. No last look at Daddy. When Willie dropped his arm from around my shoulders, I said what I had been thinking, "This casket isn't long enough for him." Willie said he had been thinking the same thing.

I remembered Mom telling me about her friend in her adopted town of Williams, Arizona—Perry Chapman, owner and director of the mortuary. His son was killed in Vietnam, but, instead of his remains, they shipped home a sealed casket full of sandbags.

So how did they fit Daddy into that standard-sized coffin? At six foot six he was not a standard-sized man. I could only imagine they had cut off his feet and tucked them inside. But of course, he died in the desert. Maybe Daddy was not in there at all. Maybe they sent sand.

***

There was little time to puzzle this out. Because Daddy and Sheila were divorced now, Daddy's stuff began to arrive at my house the next day. Boxes and boxes. Crates full of his furniture and linens and the contents of his kitchen. His work overalls and casual clothes, magazines and toothpicks evidently swept from his coffee table by someone's forearm. Rugs, curtains, bathmat and shaving cream. My ramshackle, free-standing garage filled front to back and seven feet high with cartons labeled with Daddy's name, c/o my name, from across the globe to tiny town, tiny person in Tulsa, Oklahoma.

Somehow, his storage unit in Norman emptied and trundled up the turnpike to me. Long guns, handguns. Reloading equipment. Boxes of shells and wads and pellets. Hunting vests, and competition vests with patches from the skeet range for 250 hits without a miss. More king-sized clothes. My daddy's T-shirts and tighty-whities. Size 16 work boots

and dress shoes and jump suits Grandma made for him
with 36-inch inseams, and a black-velvet dinner jacket with
satin lapels.

The wing struts, tail assembly, and dash panel, complete
with fuel gauge and altimeter, for the stunt plane he was
building now rested, as if on air, in the rafters overhead.
At least his Navion four-seater, twin-engine airplane could
remain in its hangar east of town at Harvey Young Airport.

Momma. Then Glenn. Now Daddy.

I felt alone, and so small. As each shipment arrived, I
shrank. Aware each day of the size of the sphere under my
feet and my relatively speck-like existence on it.

One night, I dreamed of standing before a large fireplace
with a stone hearth that extended up the wall all the way
to the ceiling, two, maybe even three, stories above. On the
wall were dozens of portraits, all in different frames, reaching up and out of sight at the top.

I began to study the faces closest to me and, though I did
not recognize anyone, I somehow knew, in the dream, that
these were my relatives, my ancestors, and it seemed they
were aware of me too. It gave me some small comfort; in
that moment, I felt less alone.

Then a particular picture drew my attention: A small oval
portrait of a man, perhaps from the 1880s. He is dressed in
worn wool clothes—maybe his only suit—a dress shirt, the
collar obscured by his scraggly, chest-length beard, a plaid
vest and jacket woven in a windowpane pattern. His wide-
brimmed hat is pushed back to reveal a broad forehead
with strands of his hair plastered in place and severe eyes,
light eyes. He stares fiercely back at me. Then suddenly, a

flicker, gone before it can be confirmed. Behind those eyes he laughs! He chuckles at me. The equivalent of a pat on the head. Paternal. He knows I'll be okay.

I felt better when I woke—a little lighter, not quite so small. Willie came down from Kansas and he and I began to pry crates open and sift through Daddy's stuff. We organized the first of several garage sales, placed ads that specified "king-sized" clothes, along with furniture and kitchenware. We strung clotheslines along the side of the house and lined up Daddy's enormous work boots and dress shoes below, as though we planned to clothe an invisible man. On the first day of the first sale, a short Humpty-Dumpty of a man came early and fingered the chambray shirts and elongated jumpsuits. Finally, he asked, "You advertised king-sized clothes?"

During the next weeks and months, I drove back and forth to Grandma's stuffy house in Pawnee many times to sit with her and listen while she processed her grief. She had Uncle Earl and her neighbor Rose, but she talked to me as though she had been cloistered and without companionship for many years. She started before I reached the top step, her voice low and monotone like Daddy's. "You look pretty," she would always say, as she held the screen door for me to come in. Then we would settle into our places in her crowded living room, she in her chair across from her console TV, a golf match playing just out of earshot on the murky screen, and me on the sofa to her left.

She never cried that I saw, but sometimes her words would catch, and she would have to wait before she went on to tell me what a good baby Daddy had been, or how, as

a teenager, he worked so hard at Southern Hills Country
Club to earn his own keep. She remembered when he went
into the Army and when he came home and how he wrote
to her religiously, and such beautiful letters, not just "Hi,
mom, I'm fine," like so many of them do. You could feel like
you were there with him wherever he was, see the things
he saw.

Stories flowed, not with any urgency, but as though they
came from far back in her memory and rolled into the
present without a starting point or a particular destina-
tion. Most times I did not know the people she spoke of,
except Daddy, of course, or Grandpa. I never knew "that
woman," but I knew Grandpa had strayed and they were divorced for years and remarried after a grudging forgiveness.
Grandma rarely repeated herself, but I sometimes allowed
my attention to retreat. I was tired. Weekdays, I went to
class, read my assigned chapters, wrote papers, and then
tunneled through Daddy's belongings, box by box, crate by
crate. Weekends she wore me down with these long, low,
rumbling releases.

Once, after I had determined to participate, to change the
dynamic, but failed again, I said, "Grandma, you never let
me get a word in!" and regretted it before my mouth closed.
She pulled up short and sat silent. Then, she dusted off her
lap and cut our visit short. I anguished over my impatience,
but when I called her a week later and made the trip again,
she greeted me as always, and we began to converse.

But this time, she told me stories from her life as a single
woman before Grandpa, and from during the time she and
Grandpa were apart. She asked about my life as a single

woman and the men who courted me. She sat forward and listened and advised me like a friend. I saw her in three dimensions for the first time, and maybe she saw me that way too, and I came to see that she had transferred all the attention and energy and fierce, fierce love she had for my daddy, to me. And my love for her swelled too.

When Daddy went to Dubai, he stashed his Corvette in Grandma's free-standing one-car garage in Pawnee. The walls of the tired tiny building bowed, and the doors hung lopsided on their hinges. He left the car there for safekeeping; indeed, it would be the last place a thief would look for treasure.

Grandma went out weekly at first, according to Daddy's directions, and started the engine with its throaty rumble, just to keep the fluids moving. Gradually—he lived in Dubai nearly 10 years—her routine relaxed and trailed off to fewer and fewer starts. Even before Daddy died, she quit going out there altogether.

The spring after Daddy passed, I went to the garage once more and dragged open the double doors. Daylight made a timid foray into the cramped enclosure. Brown dust had accumulated over the entire surface of the car. The tires looked low. I sidled along the driver's side, wedged myself in, wondering how Grandma had ever done it, and sat in the verboten driver's seat.

I lifted my hands and placed them where his great hands had sat, at ten and two, for maximum control. I could not help wondering what Daddy might think if he could see me there, in his place. Overhead, the liner was discolored where his hair, Brylcreemed into place, had brushed time and time again as he cruised the streets of Tulsa. The seat was so far back—as far as it could go—that my legs were fully extended, but my toes remained a full six inches from the pedals, as though to reinforce that I was in over my head, as I had been once before when I presumed to drive his car. I adjusted the seat forward and, even though the gear shift sat in neutral, I pushed in the clutch and turned the key.

To my amazement, the car started right up.

Maybe it was the engine's rumble, its deep, almost menacing thunder, its readiness to leap, that brought a reverie to the surface of that day in Tulsa, when I lived with Daddy and Sheila and was determined to defy his stifling restrictions. Why shouldn't I be allowed to drive the Corvette? I was a safe driver! I was smart. I was able. Other teenagers drove their parents' cars, though none I could think of were Corvettes. Some of my classmates had Camaros, though, and GTOs. Of course, they were all boys. Maybe that was it. He would not let me drive the car because I was a girl.

Well, you're not here to stop me now, are you? This girl knows where you keep the key and that you will not be home until hours from now.

And so, on that sunny day, I took the key, rolled up the garage door, adjusted the seat, and started the car. Incredible, the feeling. The growl, the reverberation, the power. I found reverse on the shifter but killed the engine twice before I found a balance between the unyielding clutch and gas pedals that let me ease the car back onto the slanted driveway and out into the street. Oh, my God.

The pedals were so stiff and the spring tension in them so great that I killed it again. I wondered if our neighbors were watching. A breath, and this time when I started it up, I revved the engine and thought I had let off the clutch gently, but the car catapulted into the intersection next to our house before it died again.

Okay, here we go. One more time. A tiny tremor in my hands. I needed a charm. And sure enough, I started her up, eased off the clutch, and began a slow roll down the block. Steady. Steady. But this was a long block and I did not have to go five mph all the way to that stop sign. So, I tapped the gas, just tapped it, and the car leapt half the distance to the end of the block before I could push in the clutch and coast the rest of the way.

Oh. This is why Daddy would not let me drive the car. Got it.

We sat idling back then, the Corvette and I, and reassessed our plans. I knew I would be in trouble if I tried to do more, if I went to Patti Lee's as I'd hoped, or Russell's to show off. Still, unwilling to surrender, I worked my way up and down the tree-lined blocks of Daddy and Sheila's posh neighborhood where I did not really belong, driving a car that I could barely control. And, soon enough, I eased back up the slanted driveway into the garage, returned everything to the exact place where I found it, rolled down the garage door, and went up to my room.

***

When Daddy had been gone two years, and his estate, such as it was, was settled, I tugged on the garage doors at Grandma's house again. Now the Corvette was mine and this time I would drive it back to Tulsa, a hollow victory. But when daylight seeped into the darkened space, I saw that all four tires were flat. If the car had seemed lost before, forgotten, now it sat deflated and forlorn—not dead, not dying, but succumbing nevertheless. I pushed down the urge to cry and instead felt a fleeting anger. Great. Now what?

I returned to Grandma's living room and stood limp before her, defeated, spent. But Grandma knew exactly what to do. We loaded ourselves into her Plymouth and drove to Pawnee's only service station, the Snack-N-Pak, a Conoco, and Jimbo Jones said the guy at the salvage yard south of town had an air compressor he could probably bring over. Ask for Big John.

Big John hooked his thumb into the bib of his overalls and watched as we drove onto his lot. "Nah, I can't help you right now," he said eyeing me after I explained about the flat tires, "but maybe this yahoo can. He's not much good to me." He gestured toward a gangly young man, also in overalls, and called out, "John Junior! Come 'ere!" Big John's son looked up from under the hood of a '49 Ford—a skinny spitting image of his daddy. He grinned an "aw shucks" kind of grin and loped toward me. "Yes ma'am, I can air up your tires for you! No problem at all! Let me just load up the compressor and I'll follow you back to your place."

"Mind your manners, Don Juan," Big John admonished John Junior, who actually blushed, and we set out with the young man close behind in a blue and yellow tow truck with chains swinging.

Grandma parked on the grassy sloping shoulder in front of her house and John Junior backed his tow truck toward the garage doors. He threw it into park, killed the engine, and hopped out of the cab. When I headed toward the uneven garage doors, he leapt ahead and said, "Here, let me help you with that."

We each pulled a wobbly door across the grass and gravel that made Grandma's driveway, and this time the sun flooded in, revealing the iconic split window in the Corvette's sleek fastback.

John Junior drew a breath and stood still. He exhaled, then looked at me, at Grandma, and back to the car. He shook his head and looked at me again.

"I always heard an old lady had a '63 Corvette in her garage here in town, but I never believed it. I never believed it until this day, and here I am! And here it is!"

"Yes," I agreed, "here it is."

"Do you know how much it's wor..." he began, then checked himself.

The three of us turned back to the car for a moment longer, each, I imagine, with our own thoughts about what we saw—for Grandma, the last vestige of her boy; for John Junior, a legend unveiled; and, for me, a symbol of the man I idolized and hardly knew.

***

One day when I was there, Grandma pointed to the Eastlake pump organ that stood against her dining-room wall and said, "I want you to have that." Maybe it was the next month I arrived to find she'd boxed up her china and said, "This isn't too much, but I always thought it was a pretty pattern."

She asked me to pull a chair from the dining room table and sit beside her while she went through a pasteboard box of pictures. She wanted me to have them, but not before she held each one and told me a story. We regressed, it seemed, to the speaker/audience pattern and after a time I became restless. I did not know these cousins of in-laws and I never would. But I did know I would never interrupt her again, so I steeled myself and tried not to let the need for sleep overwhelm me as she pulled out photo after photo.

"This one's Aunt Mabel from California—Hermosa Beach." And "Here's Uncle Dosier who slept on a cot in the garage all those years." The pictures got older and older the deeper she dug, and larger and more fragile. And then, "Here's my great-grandpa, James Ledford."

James Ledford, with light, piercing eyes and his hat pushed back on his head. Great-Grandpa James Ledford with a scraggly beard, in a windowpane jacket and plaid vest. James Ledford from my dream.

"Wait!" I said. "This is your grandpa?"

"He's my great-great-grandpa," she clarified. "He's not my daddy's daddy. He's my daddy's grand-daddy."

I could see him chuckling behind those keen eyes.

"That makes him my…"

"I believe that makes him your great-great-*great*-grand-pa, Honey. These are all your people," she said gesturing toward the uneven stacks of pictures. "These are your family." And in that moment, the sensation from my dream swept over me and my eyes welled. I drew a deep breath and pulled my shoulders up in wonder. Here they are! Here they are.

"Thank you, Grandma" I said. "I'll take this one for sure. I'll take them all."

***

I drove back to Tulsa that afternoon and straight to TG&Y, the local five-and-dime, where I found a frame for James Ledford's photo. I drove a nail through the lath and plaster wall and put him up in the living room, his astute and watchful eye a comfort.

James Ledford, ancestor

Chapter Thirty-One

Dawn

Glenn and I had talked about life after death, of course. We were probably high when we began a brainstorming session about a sign, something he could do from the other side that I could recognize, without a doubt, was him reaching out to me, letting me know that he was not really gone.

I do so wish we had formalized a sign.

We talked about reincarnation, Glenn and I, idly, as dabblers do. And pot smokers. He said he'd like to come back as a race car driver, "Lucky Eagle." I did not remember his having an abiding interest in car racing, but okay.

So now and then, after he was gone, I would do a search on the nickname, to no avail.

Where's my big brother? Where is Lucky Eagle?

Then I figured that if he had come back with that destiny, he would have to grow to full adulthood before he distinguished himself. So the first twenty years after his death did not matter. He could not have become Lucky Eagle so soon.

I forgot about it for a while, maybe running a cursory search every three or four years. But not too long ago, it came into my mind again, and I searched once more for race car drivers called Lucky Eagle. When nothing came up, I broadened the search to famous nicknames in professional sports, or something like that.

Before long, I was noodling around and following links almost at random. I found myself reading through a list someone at Bleacher Report had compiled of the "60 Best Nicknames in the National Hockey League." Why not? But 60? Really? And these are the best?

I was about to get a hold of myself and pay bills or do laundry or something I should be doing, when there, in the middle of the pack, down below Bob "Battleship" Kelly, Steve Buzinski "The Puck Goes Insky," and Andre "The Moose" Dupont, came "Lucky" Luc Robitaille, and then Eddie "The Eagle" Belfour, followed by Glenn "Chico" Resch.

Lucky. Eagle. Glenn.

Not one person. Not a race car driver. But who believes in reincarnation anyway? Fuck it. I say it's a sign.

Glenn and Carolyn,
c. 1953

Glenn, 1948

Lucille,
Glenn,
and
newborn
Carolyn,
1950

Family Photos

Carolyn and Glenn and their parents

Carolyn,
First Grade

Carolyn in 1953, age 3

Glenn and Carolyn, Christmas

Carolyn
and Glenn,
Christmas

The 1963 Corvette owned by Carolyn and Glenn's father traveled
to California with Carolyn and is still owned by her family.

Carolyn in 1964

Carolyn after her marriage,
April, 1971

Glenn
in his
fuzzy
orange
chair,
c. 1970

Christmss as teens; Carolyn wearing white lipstick and black eye-
iner; Glenn looking straight into the camera lens

Glenn and
his Honda

About Carolyn Plath

Born in Tulsa, Oklahoma, in 1950, Carolyn Plath earned a B.A. in education from Tulsa University and an M.A. from Northeastern. Her career in education led her from teaching English and serving as a Speech and Debate coach in Tulsa, to becoming a school principal at Glenbrook Middle School and Ygnacio Valley High School in California. She retired in 2010, continuing her love of education by offering the "Make the World a Better Place" scholarship.

Carolyn expressed her passion for writing in hundreds of columns and articles in Bay Area magazines and newspapers. Her blogs had thousands of followers from all over the world. Carolyn volunteered for local organizations: Benicia Literary Arts, Carquinez Village, and the Benicia Film Festival, to name just a few. With her husband Robert, she was known for throwing memorable parties for such occasions as the Fourth of July, Elvis Presley's birthday, and Oscar Night.

Carolyn's memoir, *Glenn's Sister*, a labor of love that she crafted with great care over the last several years, tells the story of her brother Glenn and a family secret with tragic consequences. The Benicia Literary Arts Memoir Group was lucky enough to read and critique versions of all the chapters. Three of its members have edited the book for publication to honor Carolyn as a generous and gifted fellow writer who knew she had an important story to tell.

Carolyn's passing came as a shock to all who knew her as a compassionate and energetic person with a wicked sense of humor and a penchant for fun. We, and her large community of friends, will miss her.

Notes about this book's typography

The cover title is set in Flower Power, designed by Chank Diesel of Minneapolis. His fonts were featured in the Smithsonian's Cooper-Hewitt National Design Museum as "important examples of contemporary typography."

The type for the text, Adobe Jenson Pro, was designed by Robert Slimbach of the Adobe type design team. A historical revival of Nicolas Jenson's roman and Ludovico degli Arrighi's italic typeface designs, these two icons of Renaissance type result in an elegant typeface with power and flexibility.